259

P9-CAO-053

Better Homes and Gardens®

Healthy Foods for Hungry Kids

Our seal assures you that every recipe in *Healthy Foods for Hungry Kids* has been tested in the Better Homes and Gardens® Test Kitchen. This means that each recipe is practical and reliable, and meets our high standards of taste appeal.

BETTER HOMES AND GARDENS® BOOKS

Editor: Gerald M. Knox
Art Director: Ernest Shelton
Managing Editor: David A. Kirchner
Editorial Project Managers: James D. Blume, Marsha Jahns,
    Rosanne Weber Mattson, Mary Helen Schiltz

Department Head, Cook Books: Sharyl Heiken
Associate Department Heads: Sandra Granseth,
    Rosemary C. Hutchinson, Elizabeth Woolever
Senior Food Editors: Julia Malloy, Marcia Stanley,
    Joyce Trollope
Associate Food Editors: Linda Henry, Mary Major,
    Diana McMillen, Mary Jo Plutt, Maureen Powers,
    Martha Schiel, Linda Foley Woodrum
Test Kitchen: Director, Sharon Stilwell; Photo Studio
    Director, Janet Pittman; Home Economists: Lynn Blanchard,
    Jean Brekke, Kay Cargill, Marilyn Cornelius, Jennifer
    Darling, Maryellyn Krantz, Lynelle Munn, Dianna Nolin,
    Marge Steenson

Associate Art Directors: Linda Ford Vermie, Neoma Alt West,
    Randall Yontz
Assistant Art Directors: Lynda Haupert, Harijs Priekulis,
    Tom Wegner
Senior Graphic Designers: Jack Murphy, Stan Sams,
    Darla Whipple-Frain
Graphic Designers: Mike Burns, W. Blake Welch, Brian Wignall
Art Production: Director, John Berg; Associate, Joe Heuer;
    Office Manager, Emma Rediger

President, Book Group: Fred Stines
Vice President, Retail Marketing: Jamie Martin
Vice President, Direct Marketing: Arthur Heydendael

BETTER HOMES AND GARDENS® MAGAZINE
Vice President, Editorial Director: Doris Eby
Executive Director, Editorial Services:
    Duane L. Gregg
Food and Nutrition Editor: Nancy Byal

HEALTHY FOODS FOR HUNGRY KIDS

Editor: Linda Foley Woodrum
Editorial Project Manager: James D. Blume
Graphic Designer: W. Blake Welch
Electronic Text Processor: Paula Forest
Food Stylists: Janet Pittman, Judy Tills
Contributing Photographers: Ron Crofoot,
    Mike Dieter, M. Jensen Photography, Inc.,
    Scott Little
Contributing Illustrator: Steve Shock

On the cover: Mix-and-Match Multigrain Pizza
(see recipe, page 42)

© Copyright 1987 by Meredith Corporation, Des Moines, Iowa.
All Rights Reserved. Printed in the United States of America.
First Edition. First Printing.
Library of Congress Catalog Card Number: 86-61620
ISBN: 0-696-01691-5 (hard cover)
ISBN: 0-696-01690-7 (trade paperback)

Contents

The Peepers
Food has to look good for kids to give it a chance.

The Sniffer
Don't forget their noses. The aroma of food determines how well kids will accept it.

The Taster
Once you get the food past the kids' eyes and noses, their taste buds give it the true test.

The Throwers
Something as simple as throwing a ball is difficult without energy from nourishing foods.

This Is a Kid

His name is Jimmy. Like most kids, Jimmy often turns up his nose at foods that are good for him. Yet he needs healthy foods for energy to work, play, study, and even sleep.

We developed the recipes in *Healthy Foods for Hungry Kids* with kids like Jimmy in mind. Not only are the recipes good for kids (and the entire family), but they taste good, too. And to prove it, we had dozens of kids try the recipes to make sure they liked what they saw, smelled, and, most important, tasted. If the kids didn't like it, it's not in this book.

But don't take our word for it. Check out the kid quotes throughout the book. Straight from the kids to you . . . this cookbook is the answer to feeding your family right.

The Jumpers
Eating the right foods gives kids energy to play hard.

The Runners
Every step is easy when kids eat a variety of foods that are good for them.

"good stuff!"

Jessica, age 10
(see recipe, page 44)

"yummy!"

Ryan, age 7
(see recipe, page 58)

"mmmm"

Caitlin, age 5
(see recipe, page 18)

Alpha-Bet Cakes

¾ cup whole wheat flour ½ cup all-purpose flour 2 tablespoons brown sugar 1 teaspoon baking powder ¼ teaspoon baking soda	● In a medium mixing bowl stir together whole wheat flour, all-purpose flour, sugar, baking powder, and baking soda.	**First designer jeans, now designer pancakes! Personalize the morning hotcakes with your kids' initials or a special shape. We guarantee rave reviews for this latest fad.**
1 beaten egg 1½ cups buttermilk 1 tablespoon cooking oil	● Combine egg, buttermilk, and oil. Add all at once to the flour mixture. Stir till combined but still slightly lumpy.	
	● For each pancake, carefully spoon ¼ to ½ cup batter onto a hot, lightly greased griddle or heavy skillet to form a letter or shape (for example, initials, bunny, bear, turtle, car, cat, funny face, snowman, flower, or star).	**To make sure your griddle or skillet is hot enough, heat it over medium heat till drops of water dance across the surface.**
Reduced-calorie pancake and waffle syrup	● Cook till golden brown, turning when pancakes have bubbly surfaces and slightly dry edges. Serve with syrup. Makes about nine 4-inch pancakes.	

Wacky Waffles

1 cup whole wheat flour
¾ cup all-purpose flour
1 tablespoon baking powder
¼ teaspoon ground nutmeg
1 ripe medium banana
1 beaten egg
1¾ cups milk
2 tablespoons cooking oil

● In a large mixing bowl stir together flours, baking powder, nutmeg, and dash *salt*. Mash banana. In a medium mixing bowl stir mashed banana, *egg*, milk, and oil with a fork till combined. Add to flour mixture all at once. Stir till mixture is combined but still slightly lumpy.

What's so wacky about these waffles? They have a secret flavor hidden in the whole grain batter. We'll give you a hint: Monkeys would love them.

¾ cup finely chopped pecans

● Pour *½ cup* batter onto grids of a preheated, lightly greased waffle baker. Sprinkle *2 tablespoons* nuts over batter. Close lid; don't open during baking. Bake till steam stops escaping from sides. Use a fork to lift waffle off grid. Repeat with remaining batter and nuts.

Jam-Time Berries
Vanilla *or* fruit-flavored
  low-fat yogurt (optional)

● To keep waffles warm, place in a single layer on a wire rack placed on a baking sheet. Set in a warm oven. Serve with Jam-Time Berries and yogurt, if desired. Makes six 7-inch-round or three 9-inch-square waffles.

Jam-Time Berries: In a mixing bowl mash 4 cups fresh or thawed frozen *raspberries, blueberries,* or *strawberries*. Stir in ½ cup *honey*. Makes 3 cups.

Eggstra-Special Scramble

3 eggs
3 tablespoons milk
1 tablespoon snipped
   parsley
   Dash ground nutmeg

● In a medium mixing bowl beat together eggs, milk, parsley, and nutmeg with a fork; set aside.

Brandy, one of our kid testers, thought this tasted like a scrambled-eggs-and-apple-pie breakfast. No wonder. It's loaded with eggs, apples, and cheddar cheese.

1 tablespoon margarine
1 small apple, cored and
   chopped (¾ cup)

● In a medium skillet melt margarine over medium heat; add apple. Cook and stir for 2 to 3 minutes or till just tender. Pour in egg mixture. Cook without stirring till mixture just begins to set on the bottom and around the edges.

¼ cup shredded cheddar *or*
   Monterey Jack cheese
   (1 ounce)

● Then, to scramble, using a large spoon or spatula, lift and fold partially cooked eggs so uncooked portion flows underneath. Continue cooking and gently folding about 3 minutes more or till eggs are cooked throughout but still glossy and moist. Remove from heat. Sprinkle with cheese. Makes 2 servings.

Microwave Method: Beat together eggs, milk, parsley, and nutmeg with a fork; set aside. In a 7-inch microwave-safe pie plate micro-cook margarine on 100% power (high) for 20 to 30 seconds or till melted. Add apple. Cook, uncovered, on high for 1 to 1½ minutes or till apple is just tender, stirring once.

Pour in egg mixture. Micro-cook, uncovered, on 50% power (medium) for 4 to 5 minutes or till eggs are nearly set, pushing cooked portions to center of dish several times during cooking. Sprinkle with cheese.

Peanut Butter And Jelly Oatmeal

3 cups water
1½ cups quick-cooking rolled oats

● In a medium saucepan bring water to boiling. Slowly add oats, stirring constantly. Cook, stirring occasionally, for 1 minute. Cover. Remove from heat and let stand for 3 minutes.

¼ cup peanut butter
¼ cup jelly *or* jam
Milk (optional)

● Spoon peanut butter and jelly or jam onto individual servings; stir to swirl. Add milk, if desired. Makes 4 or 5 servings.

You don't have to wait till lunch to enjoy peanut butter and jelly. Jump the gun and swirl some peanut butter and jelly or jam into hot cooked oatmeal.

Overnight Oatmeal

3 cups apple juice *or* cider
1⅓ cups regular rolled oats
¼ cup raisins *or* snipped dried apricots
1 tablespoon unprocessed wheat bran
2 teaspoons toasted wheat germ
¼ teaspoon ground cinnamon

● In a 4-cup airtight container combine apple juice or cider, rolled oats, raisins or apricots, wheat bran, wheat germ, and cinnamon. Cover and store in the refrigerator up to 3 days. Makes enough for 4 servings.

Put this oatmeal to bed in the refrigerator and wake up to ready-to-heat-and-eat oatmeal. It's as easy as instant!

To make 1 serving: In a small saucepan place about *1 cup* cereal mixture. Bring just to boiling. Reduce heat and simmer, uncovered, for 5 minutes, stirring occasionally. (Or place cereal mixture in a microwave-safe bowl. Cover loosely with waxed paper. Micro-cook on 100% power [high] for 2½ to 3 minutes or till heated through, stirring every minute.)

Four-Grain Cereal

½ cup regular rolled oats
½ cup quick-cooking barley
½ cup cracked wheat
½ cup sunflower nuts *or* slivered almonds, toasted
½ cup raisins *or* chopped pitted dates
¼ cup millet

● In a 3-cup airtight storage container stir together rolled oats, barley, cracked wheat, nuts, raisins or dates, and millet. Cover and store at room temperature up to 1 month. Makes about 2¾ cups or enough for 8 servings.

Question: What tasty breakfast cereal contains rolled oats, barley, cracked wheat, and millet, all in one bite?

Answer: Four-Grain Cereal.

To make 1 serving: In a small saucepan bring ⅓ cup *apple juice or water* to boiling. Stir in *3 tablespoons* cereal mixture. Cover and simmer for 12 to 15 minutes or to desired consistency. Serve with *milk* and *honey or reduced-calorie pancake and waffle syrup.*

To make 4 servings: In a 2-quart saucepan bring 1⅓ cups *apple juice or water* to boiling. Stir in *¾ cup* cereal mixture. Cover and simmer 15 minutes or to desired consistency. Serve as above.

Giddyap Granola

2½ cups regular rolled oats
½ cup slivered almonds
½ cup coconut
½ cup toasted wheat germ
½ cup sesame seed
½ cup sunflower nuts
½ cup dark corn syrup *or* honey
⅓ cup orange juice

● In an extra-large mixing bowl combine oats, almonds, coconut, wheat germ, sesame seed, and sunflower nuts.

Stir together syrup or honey and orange juice. Pour over oat mixture, stirring till coated. Spread mixture evenly in a greased 15x10x1-inch baking pan. Bake in a 300° oven for 45 to 50 minutes or till brown, first stirring every 15 minutes, then several times during the last 15 minutes.

½ cup raisins (optional)

● Remove from oven. Stir in raisins, if desired. Transfer mixture to another pan. Cool. Store in an airtight container up to 1 month. Makes about 5 cups.

This oil-free granola will help any droopy-eyed cowpoke "giddyap" in the morning.

Rise-and-Shine Refrigerator Muffins

1 cup all-purpose flour
¾ cup unprocessed wheat
    bran
½ cup whole wheat flour
2½ teaspoons baking powder
½ teaspoon ground
    cinnamon
¼ teaspoon salt
¼ teaspoon ground nutmeg

● In a large mixing bowl stir together all-purpose flour, bran, whole wheat flour, baking powder, cinnamon, salt, and nutmeg. Make a well in the center.

There's nothing better than fresh hot muffins for breakfast, especially if they're a cinch to make. Just keep this batter in the refrigerator, then dip into it and bake as many nutty muffins as you like.

2 beaten eggs
1 cup milk
⅓ cup packed brown sugar
⅓ cup cooking oil
⅓ cup raisins *or* chopped
    pitted dates
⅓ cup sunflower nuts *or*
    chopped pecans *or*
    walnuts

● In a medium mixing bowl combine eggs, milk, sugar, and oil; add all at once to flour mixture, stirring just till moistened (batter should be thick and lumpy). Fold in raisins or dates and nuts. Use batter immediately or store in a covered container in the refrigerator up to 5 days.

● To bake, gently stir batter. Grease desired number of muffin cups or line with paper bake cups; fill ⅔ full. Bake in a 400° oven for 15 to 18 minutes or till brown. Makes up to 15 muffins.

Microwave Method: Prepare Rise-and-Shine Refrigerator Muffins as above, *except* line one or two 6-ounce custard cups with a paper bake cup. Spoon 3 tablespoons batter into each.

For one muffin, micro-cook on 100% power (high) for 30 to 50 seconds or till done. (Scratch the slightly wet surface with a wooden toothpick. The muffin should be cooked underneath.) For two muffins, cook for 50 to 60 seconds. Let stand for 5 minutes.

Attention, Microwave Owners

Recipes with microwave directions were tested in countertop microwave ovens that operate on 600 to 700 watts. Times are approximate because microwave ovens vary by manufacturer.

TAKE·ALONG LUNCHES

Everyone needs a tummy-filling lunch to get through the afternoon—kids especially. But there's not always time to pack noontime necessities during a busy morning. Relax. To help ease the A.M. rat race, we've come up with a chapter full of nutritious sandwiches to make ahead and store in the freezer. In the morning, simply grab a sandwich from the freezer and pack it in a brown bag or lunch box. The frozen sandwich will thaw by lunchtime.

But before you send your child out the door with brown bag in hand, keep these lunch-toting tips in mind:
● Some recipes recommend packing a box of frozen juice with the sandwich in the morning. This keeps the sandwich from thawing too quickly. At lunchtime, your kids can enjoy cold sandwiches and chilled or slushy juice.
● Make sure your kids don't set their lunches in a warm place, such as near a hot radiator or a sunny window.
● Freezing sandwiches is unnecessary if kids store their lunches in a refrigerator.

Telescope Roll-Ups

3 tablespoons plain low-fat yogurt
3 tablespoons mayonnaise *or* salad dressing
2 teaspoons soy sauce
1 teaspoon prepared mustard
¼ teaspoon onion powder
6 ounces tofu (fresh bean curd), drained and mashed (1 cup)
¾ cup shredded Colby *or* cheddar cheese (3 ounces)
¼ cup chopped peanuts, pecans, *or* walnuts

● In a mixing bowl stir together yogurt, mayonnaise or salad dressing, soy sauce, mustard, and onion powder. Stir in tofu, cheese, and nuts.

You won't get a peek at a comet by looking through our telescope sandwiches. Take a bite, though, for a mouthful of tasty eggless egg salad. The flavor is out of this world.

12 slices soft whole wheat bread
Margarine

● Trim crusts from bread. Roll each slice of bread lightly with a rolling pin. Spread bread lightly with margarine. Spread about *2 tablespoons* tofu mixture on *each* slice of bread.

To assemble sandwiches, spread each prepared slice of bread with the filling. Roll up the bread slice from one of the long sides. The ends of the bread will barely overlap.

● Roll up bread slices. Place, seam side down, in an 11x7x1½-inch or 9x9x2-inch baking pan. Freeze about 1 hour or till firm. Remove sandwiches from the pan. Seal, label, and freeze. Store up to 1 month in the freezer. Makes 12 sandwiches or 6 servings.

● For *each* serving, in the morning pack *2 frozen* roll-ups in a brown bag or lunch box with a frozen box of juice. Roll-ups will thaw in 4 to 6 hours.

Tuna Canoes

¼ cup plain low-fat yogurt
2 tablespoons mayonnaise
  or salad dressing
1 teaspoon prepared
  mustard
¼ teaspoon dried dillweed
  Dash pepper
	● In a medium mixing bowl stir together yogurt, mayonnaise or salad dressing, mustard, dillweed, and pepper.

1 6½-ounce can tuna
  (water pack), drained
  and flaked
⅓ cup chopped red sweet
  pepper, carrot, *or* celery
2 frankfurter buns, split
½ cup shredded cheddar
  cheese (2 ounces)
	● Stir tuna and red pepper, carrot, or celery into yogurt mixture.
	  Use a fork to hollow out the tops and bottoms of buns, leaving ¼-inch shells. Sprinkle cheese into hollowed-out buns. Spoon tuna mixture over cheese. Seal, label, and freeze. Store up to 1 month in the freezer. Makes 4 sandwiches.

	● For *each* serving, in the morning pack *1 frozen* sandwich in a brown bag or lunch box with a frozen box of juice. The sandwich will thaw in 4 to 5 hours.

Paddle one of these tuna sandwiches into your mouth for a tasty lunchtime voyage. To help keep your tuna cargo cold, pack it with a frozen box of fruit juice.

Sprinkle shredded cheese into the hollowed-out frankfurter buns. Then spoon the tuna mixture over the cheese. The cheese prevents the bread from getting soggy.

Phony Baloney Sandwiches

¼ cup plain low-fat yogurt
2 tablespoons mayonnaise
  or salad dressing
¼ teaspoon curry powder *or*
  1 teaspoon prepared
  mustard
	● In a small mixing bowl stir together yogurt, mayonnaise or salad dressing, and curry powder or mustard.

1 cup finely chopped turkey
  bologna
¼ cup shredded carrot
¼ cup raisins *or* currants
¼ cup chopped celery
  Margarine
6 slices whole grain bread
	● Stir bologna, carrot, raisins or currants, and celery into yogurt mixture. Spread margarine on one side of each slice of bread. Spread bologna mixture on 3 of the bread slices. Top with remaining bread. Halve sandwiches. Seal, label, and freeze. Store up to 1 month in the freezer. Makes 3 sandwiches.

	● For *each* serving, in the morning pack *1 frozen* sandwich in a brown bag or lunch box with a frozen box of juice. The sandwich will thaw in 4 to 5 hours.

The kids who eagerly gobbled up these sandwiches thought the phony baloney (turkey bologna) was the real McCoy. Little did they know that turkey bologna has 33% less fat than beef or pork bologna.

Champion Chicken Pitas

¼ **cup plain low-fat yogurt**
¼ **cup buttermilk**
   salad dressing

● In a small bowl stir together yogurt and buttermilk salad dressing.

1½ **cups diced cooked**
   chicken *or* **turkey**
½ **cup chopped broccoli** *or*
   green pepper
¼ **cup shredded carrot**
¼ **cup chopped pecans** *or*
   walnuts
 2 **large whole wheat pita**
   bread rounds, halved
   crosswise
   Margarine

● In a medium mixing bowl combine chicken or turkey, broccoli or green pepper, carrot, and nuts. Add the yogurt mixture; stir well. Spread insides of pita halves with margarine; spoon chicken mixture into pita halves. Seal, label, and freeze. Store up to 1 month in the freezer. Makes 4 sandwiches.

Take it from our fine feathered friend (Champion Chicken, that is), this sandwich is a winner. The low-fat yogurt dressing qualifies it for the lightweight division. After one bite you'll agree, it's a knockout!

● For *each* serving, in the morning pack *1 frozen* pita half in a brown bag or a lunch box with one frozen box of juice. The sandwich will thaw in 4 to 5 hours.

Peanut Butter Blitz

¾ cup peanut butter
⅓ cup unsweetened
    applesauce
¼ cup raisins
    Dash ground cinnamon
8 slices whole grain bread

● In a bowl stir together peanut butter, applesauce, raisins, and cinnamon.
   Spread peanut butter mixture on *four* slices of bread. Top with remaining slices. Seal, label, and freeze, if desired. Store sandwiches up to 1 month in the freezer. Makes 4 sandwiches.

● For *each* serving, in the morning pack *1 frozen* sandwich in a brown bag or lunch box. The sandwich will thaw in about 2 hours.

Banana Peanut Butter: Stir together ¾ cup *peanut butter* and 1 chopped small *banana*. Assemble, store, and carry as above.

Crunchy Peanut Butter: Stir together ¾ cup *peanut butter* and ½ cup finely chopped *celery*. Assemble, store, and carry as above.

Tropical Peanut Butter: Stir together ⅔ cup *peanut butter*, one 8-ounce can drained crushed *pineapple*, and ¼ cup *coconut*. Assemble, store, and carry as above.

Apple Peanut Butter: Stir together ¾ cup *peanut butter*, 1 chopped *apple*, and ½ cup shredded Colby *cheese*. Assemble, store, and carry as above.

Flying Saucer Sandwiches

1 cup chopped cooked lean beef ½ cup shredded carrot 1 3-ounce package cream cheese with chives, softened 3 tablespoons milk 2 tablespoons sweet pickle relish ⅛ teaspoon pepper	● In a medium mixing bowl stir together beef, carrot, cream cheese, milk, pickle relish, and pepper. Set aside.
1 10-ounce package refrigerated whole wheat bread dough	● Divide dough into 8 portions. On a lightly floured surface roll each portion into a 5-inch circle.
Milk	● Place about ⅓ *cup* beef mixture onto *each* of *four* circles of dough. Moisten edge of dough with milk. Place remaining dough on top, stretching to fit bottom circles. Seal edges with a fork.
Milk	● Place on a greased baking sheet. Prick tops and brush with milk. Bake in a 375° oven for 15 to 20 minutes or till golden brown. Remove from baking sheet. Cool on a wire rack. Seal, label, and freeze. Store up to 1 month in the freezer. Makes 4 sandwiches.
	● For *each* serving, in the morning pack *1 frozen* sandwich in a brown bag or lunch box with a frozen box of juice. The sandwich will thaw in 4 to 6 hours.

Stomach to mouth, stomach to mouth: Send down another bite of that UFO (undeniably fantastic object).

When you pack this frozen sandwich for lunch, wrap it in a napkin. As the sandwich thaws, the napkin will absorb any moisture on the crust.

Seven-Grain Sandwich Bread

2 cups boiling water ⅓ cup seven-grain cereal ¼ cup margarine ¼ cup honey	● In a large mixer bowl pour boiling water over cereal. Add margarine and honey; stir till margarine melts. Let cool to lukewarm (115° to 120°).	**Add fiber to your kids' sandwiches with homemade whole grain bread. Seven-grain cereal (found in health food stores) is a mixture of wheat, rye, corn, barley, oat, soy, and buckwheat.**
5 to 5½ cups all-purpose flour ⅓ cup nonfat dry milk powder ⅓ cup toasted wheat germ 2 packages active dry yeast 1 teaspoon salt 2 eggs	● In a mixing bowl combine *2 cups* of the flour, dry milk powder, wheat germ, yeast, and salt. Add to cereal mixture; add eggs.	
½ cup sunflower nuts ⅓ cup quick-cooking rolled oats ⅓ cup yellow cornmeal	● Beat with an electric mixer on low speed for 30 seconds, scraping sides of bowl constantly. Beat on high speed for 3 minutes. Stir in sunflower nuts, oats, and cornmeal.	
	● Using a spoon, stir in as much remaining flour as you can. Turn dough out onto a lightly floured surface. Knead in enough of the remaining flour to make a moderately stiff dough that is smooth and elastic (6 to 8 minutes total). Shape into a ball. Place in a lightly greased bowl; turn once. Cover; let rise till double (45 to 50 minutes).	
Yellow cornmeal *or* **quick-cooking rolled oats** **Milk**	● Punch dough down; divide in half. Cover and let rest for 10 minutes. Grease two 9x5x3-inch loaf pans; lightly sprinkle bottoms and sides with more cornmeal or oats. Shape dough into 2 loaves. Place in prepared loaf pans. Brush surface lightly with milk and sprinkle with cornmeal or rolled oats. Cover and let rise till nearly double (about 30 minutes). Bake in a 375° oven about 40 minutes or till brown, covering with foil about halfway through to prevent overbrowning, if necessary. Remove from pans immediately. Cool on a wire rack. Makes 2 loaves.	

Sprouted-Wheat Bread

2½ to 3 cups all-purpose flour 2 cups whole wheat flour 1 teaspoon salt	● In a large mixer bowl stir together *1 cup* of the all-purpose flour, *1 cup* of the whole wheat flour, and salt.	**If you don't have sprouted wheat or rye berries, use millet. Our junior tester Jeremy preferred nutty-tasting wheat berries, but Amanda liked the crunch of the millet.**
1½ cups warm water (115° to 120°) ⅓ cup honey 1 package active dry yeast 2 tablespoons cooking oil	● In a mixing bowl combine water, honey, and yeast; mix till yeast dissolves. Stir in oil. Add to flour mixture. Beat with an electric mixer on low speed for 30 seconds, scraping sides of bowl. Beat on high speed for 3 minutes.	
1 cup sprouted wheat *or* rye berries (see directions, pages 68-70) *or* ½ cup millet	● Stir in sprouted berries or millet. Using a spoon, stir in remaining whole wheat flour and as much remaining all-purpose flour as you can.	
	● Turn out onto a lightly floured surface. Knead in enough remaining all-purpose flour to make a moderately stiff dough that is smooth and elastic (6 to 8 minutes total). Shape into a ball. Place in a lightly greased bowl; turn once to grease surface. Cover and let rise in a warm place till double (about 1 hour).	
	● Punch dough down. Divide in half. Cover; let rest for 10 minutes. Shape into loaves. Place in greased 8x4x2-inch loaf pans. Cover; let rise till nearly double (about 1 hour).	
	● Bake in a 375° oven for 35 to 40 minutes or till brown. Cover loaves with foil the last 15 minutes to prevent overbrowning. Remove from pans; cool on a wire rack. Makes 2 loaves.	

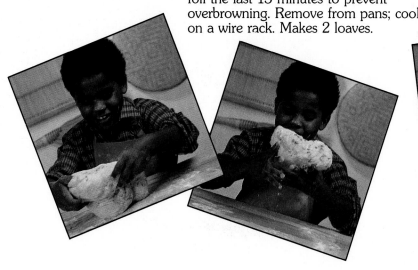

Parmesan Seasoning

Taco Seasoning

Cheese Seasoning

POP

Pick-and-Choose Popcorn

4 to 6 cups popped corn (about ¼ cup unpopped)
   Parmesan, Taco, *or* Cheese Seasoning

● Place popped corn in a large mixing bowl. Toss with Parmesan, Taco, or Cheese Seasoning. Serves 4 to 6.

Parmesan Seasoning: Stir together 2 tablespoons melted *margarine*, 2 tablespoons grated *Parmesan cheese*, and 1 tablespoon finely snipped *parsley*. Toss with warm popped popcorn.

Taco Seasoning: Stir together 2 tablespoons melted *margarine* and 1 teaspoon *taco seasoning mix*. Toss with warm popped popcorn.

Cheese Seasoning: Stir together 2 tablespoons melted *margarine* and 1 tablespoon *grated American cheese food*. Toss with warm popped popcorn.

Pop up a trio of taste tempters: Parmesan, Taco, and Cheese Popcorn. One of our food editors dropped some Cheese Popcorn into the Taco Popcorn and voilà— Taco-Cheese Popcorn!

Honey 'n' Spice Popcorn

10 cups popped corn (about ⅓ cup unpopped)
 1 cup peanuts
 ¼ cup honey
 3 tablespoons margarine
 1 teaspoon finely shredded orange peel (optional)
 ¼ teaspoon ground cinnamon

● Place popped corn and peanuts in a large roasting pan. In a small saucepan combine honey, margarine, orange peel (if desired), and cinnamon. Heat and stir till margarine melts. Pour over popcorn and nuts, tossing to coat.

● Bake in a 300° oven for 30 minutes, stirring about every 10 minutes. Transfer to a baking sheet or sheet of foil; cool. Makes about 10 cups.

A touch of honey and spice makes everything nice, especially popcorn. That's why this subtle sweet snack is lightly coated with only a touch of the honey mixture.

Grab-and-Go Mix

2 cups dried banana chips,
   or apples *or* apricots,
   quartered
1 cup corn bran cereal,
   round toasted oat
   cereal, *or* bite-size
   wheat, rice, corn,
   or bran square cereal
1 cup peanuts *or*
   unblanched whole
   almonds
½ cup pumpkin seed
   (optional)

● In a plastic bag combine fruit, cereal, nuts, and pumpkin seed, if desired. Close bag and shake well. Store in the closed bag or in an airtight container up to 1 month. Makes about 4 cups.

When we asked kid tester Adam whether he would grab a handful of this on the run, he said no. He said he'd stick around and eat the whole batch!

Hidden-Fruit Treasures

¼ cup peanut butter
2 tablespoons nonfat dry
   milk powder
2 tablespoons toasted wheat
   germ
1 tablespoon honey
   Dried banana chips,
   apricot halves, *or* other
   fruit

● In a small mixing bowl stir together peanut butter, milk powder, wheat germ, and honey. Press about 1 teaspoon peanut butter mixture completely around 1 piece of dried fruit. (Or stir 2 tablespoons snipped *dried fruit* into the peanut butter mixture and serve on crackers.) Chill in refrigerator. Serves 4.

Aye, mateys! The search for the delicious (and nutritious) treasure stops here. Pop one of these peanut butter bundles into your mouth and you will discover the fruity surprise that waits inside.

Dried Fruit Leather

8 ounces dried apples, pears, peaches, apricots, *or* mixed fruit **1½ cups water**	● In a medium saucepan combine dried fruit and water. Bring to boiling; reduce heat. Cover and simmer apples about 15 minutes, or pears, peaches, apricots, or mixed fruit about 30 minutes, or till fruit is very tender. Drain off liquid, if necessary. Cool. (Remove pits from prunes if using mixed fruit.)	**Who would eat leather? Kids! We couldn't pull our kid testers away from this chewy fruit snack.**
Nonstick spray coating	● Blend fruit in a blender or food processor. Line a 15x10x1-inch baking pan with foil; spray with nonstick coating. Spread fruit in a *thin even* layer over foil. Place in a 300° oven for 25 minutes. Without opening door, turn off oven and let dry 8 hours or overnight.	
	● Lift foil and fruit leather out of baking pan. Remove fruit leather from foil. Roll up fruit leather from one of the short sides; wrap in moisture- and vaporproof wrap. Store in the refrigerator up to 3 months or in the freezer up to 6 months. To serve, unroll and tear off pieces as desired. Makes one 10-inch roll.	

Spray a foil-lined baking pan with nonstick coating to prevent sticking. Pour fruit mixture onto pan. Using a rubber scraper, spread in a thin even layer over the foil.

When fruit leather is dry, remove it from the foil by holding foil with one hand and peeling fruit leather off foil with your other hand.

Playmate Pizzas

3 whole wheat English muffins *or* bagels, split and toasted
¾ cup shredded cheddar cheese (3 ounces)
1 8-ounce can tomato sauce
4 *or* 5 slices Canadian-style bacon
1 2½-ounce jar sliced mushrooms, drained, *or* ½ cup pitted ripe olives, sliced

● Sprinkle toasted muffins or bagels with cheese. Spread tomato sauce over cheese. Cut Canadian-style bacon to make 6 mouths and 12 eyes. Arrange mouths and eyes on muffins. Arrange mushrooms or olives around the top edge to resemble hair.

Place pizzas on a baking sheet. Bake in a 450° oven about 5 minutes or till hot. Makes 6 servings.

Go ahead and make the pizza faces happy or sad. Either way, one bite is sure to put a smile on *your* face.

Crunch-Top Banana Loaf

2 cups bite-size bran
   square cereal
¾ cup chopped walnuts
1 tablespoon brown sugar
1 tablespoon margarine,
   melted

● Crush cereal with a rolling pin to make 1 cup crumbs. For cereal topping, combine ¼ *cup* of the cereal crumbs, ¼ *cup* of the walnuts, brown sugar, and melted margarine. Set aside.

Be sure to press the cereal topping lightly into the batter so it stays on top of the baked bread.

⅔ cup sugar
⅓ cup margarine
1 egg
3 ripe medium bananas,
   mashed (1 cup)
½ cup buttermilk
1 cup all-purpose flour
1 cup whole wheat flour
2 teaspoons baking powder
½ teaspoon baking soda
¼ teaspoon salt

● In a large mixer bowl beat sugar and margarine till fluffy. Add egg, bananas, and buttermilk; beat till well combined. Stir together all-purpose flour, whole wheat flour, baking powder, baking soda, and salt. Add to creamed mixture; beat till well combined. Fold in remaining crushed crumbs and nuts.

● Transfer batter to a greased 9x5x3-inch loaf pan. Sprinkle with cereal topping, lightly pressing into batter. Bake in a 350° oven for 55 to 60 minutes or till a wooden toothpick inserted near the center comes out clean. Cover with foil the last 10 minutes to prevent overbrowning. Cool 10 minutes. Remove from pan; cool. Makes 1 loaf.

Cheese 'n' Fruit Spread

1 8-ounce container
   reduced-calorie soft-
   style cream cheese
½ cup unsweetened
   pineapple juice
½ cup dried fruit, finely
   snipped

● In a mixing bowl stir together cream cheese and pineapple juice till smooth. Add snipped fruit; mix well. Cover and chill overnight. Serve with crackers, bread, or bagels. Cover and store in the refrigerator up to 1 week. Makes 2 cups.

Fight off stomach growls with this creamy spread. You'll be armed with a healthy mixture of cream cheese, fruit juice, and dried fruit.

Whole Wheat Pretzels

2 to 2½ cups all-purpose flour
1 package active dry yeast
1½ cups milk
¼ cup packed brown sugar
2 tablespoons cooking oil
½ teaspoon salt

● In a mixer bowl combine *1½ cups* of the all-purpose flour and yeast. In a saucepan heat milk, brown sugar, oil, and salt till warm (115° to 120°), stirring constantly. Add to all-purpose flour mixture. Beat with an electric mixer on low speed for 30 seconds, scraping sides of bowl. Beat on high for 3 minutes.

2 cups whole wheat flour
¼ cup chopped sunflower nuts

● Using a spoon, stir in whole wheat flour, sunflower nuts, and as much of the remaining all-purpose flour as you can. Turn out onto a lightly floured surface. Knead in enough of the remaining all-purpose flour to make a moderately stiff dough that is smooth and elastic (6 to 8 minutes total). Shape into a ball. Place in a lightly greased bowl; turn once. Cover; let rise till double (about 1½ hours).

● Punch dough down. Cover; let rest for 10 minutes. On a lightly floured surface roll dough into a 12x10-inch rectangle. Cut into twenty 12x½-inch strips. Gently pull each strip into a rope about 16 inches long. Shape into pretzels, as shown. Place on greased baking sheets. Bake in a 475° oven for 4 minutes; remove from oven. Set oven to 350°.

1 teaspoon salt
3 quarts boiling water

● Dissolve salt in boiling water. Lower 3 or 4 pretzels at a time into boiling water; boil 2 minutes, turning once. Using a slotted spoon, transfer to paper towels; let stand a few seconds. Place pretzels ½ inch apart on well-greased baking sheets. Repeat with remaining pretzels.

1 slightly beaten egg white (optional)
1 tablespoon water (optional)
¼ cup chopped sunflower nuts

● If desired, stir together egg white and water. Brush pretzels with egg-white mixture. Sprinkle with sunflower nuts. Bake in the 350° oven for 25 to 30 minutes or till brown. Remove and cool on a wire rack. Makes 20 pretzels.

Honey-Orange Pretzels: Prepare Whole Wheat Pretzels as directed at left, *except* substitute *orange juice* for milk, *honey* for sugar, and omit sunflower nuts. Add ¼ cup dried *currants* or chopped *raisins* and ½ teaspoon finely shredded *orange peel* to the dough. Omit the salt from the boiling water. (Note: you may need more all-purpose flour.) If desired, sprinkle lightly with sugar before the final baking.

Buttermilk-Rye Pretzels: Prepare Whole Wheat Pretzels as directed at left, *except* use 2½ to 3 cups all-purpose flour and substitute *buttermilk* for milk and 1½ cups *rye flour* for whole wheat flour. Omit sunflower nuts and add 1 tablespoon *caraway seed* to dough. If desired, sprinkle lightly with salt before the final baking time.

Honey-Orange Pretzels

Whole Wheat Pretzels

Buttermilk-Rye Pretzels

Granola Muffins

1 cup Giddyap Granola (see recipe, page 12) *or* purchased granola ½ cup snipped dried apricots *or* raisins ½ cup boiling water	● In a small mixing bowl combine granola and apricots or raisins. Pour boiling water over mixture; set aside.
1 cup all-purpose flour ¾ cup whole wheat flour ⅓ cup sugar 1 tablespoon baking powder	● In a medium mixing bowl stir together all-purpose flour, whole wheat flour, sugar, and baking powder. Make a well in the center.
1 beaten egg ⅔ cup milk ⅓ cup cooking oil	● Stir together egg, milk, and oil. Stir in granola mixture. Add all at once to flour mixture, stirring just till moistened (batter should be lumpy).
Granola	● Grease muffin cups or line with paper bake cups; fill ¾ full. Sprinkle with additional granola. Bake in a 375° oven for 20 to 25 minutes or till brown. Makes about 18 muffins.

When filling the muffin cups, use an ice-cream scoop for better control. Use a ¼-cup ice-cream scoop to fill the muffin cups ¾ full.

Jelly-in-the-Belly Muffins

1 cup all-purpose flour 1 cup whole wheat flour ¼ cup packed brown sugar 2 teaspoons baking powder ¼ teaspoon baking soda ¼ teaspoon salt	● In a large mixing bowl stir together all-purpose flour, whole wheat flour, sugar, baking powder, baking soda, and salt. Make a well in the center.
1 beaten egg 1 cup buttermilk ¼ cup cooking oil 2 tablespoons chopped walnuts	● In a small bowl stir together egg, buttermilk, and oil. Add all at once to flour mixture, stirring just till moistened (batter should be lumpy). Fold in nuts.
2 tablespoons jam *or* jelly	● Grease muffin cups or line with paper bake cups. Spoon *2 tablespoons* batter into each muffin cup. Make a slight indentation in batter. Place *½ teaspoon* jam or jelly in *each* indentation; top with *1 tablespoon* batter. Bake in a 400° oven for 20 to 25 minutes or till brown. Makes 12 muffins.

You'll find touches of gooey jelly in the bellies of these whole grain muffins. The muffins will satisfy kids' jelly urges without overdoing it.

Wholesome Oat Crackers

1 cup quick-cooking rolled oats ⅔ cup all-purpose flour ⅓ cup toasted wheat germ 1 tablespoon brown sugar ½ teaspoon salt, seasoned salt, celery salt, *or* garlic salt	● In a large mixing bowl stir together oats, flour, wheat germ, sugar, and desired salt. Make a well in the center.	**Each crispy cracker is packed with fiber (thanks to rolled oats and wheat germ) and lean on sugar and fat. Kid tester Andy thought they'd be good spread with peanut butter.**
½ cup water 2 tablespoons cooking oil	● Add water and oil all at once to flour mixture, stirring till dry ingredients are moistened. Form dough into a ball; divide in half.	
	● Between 2 sheets of clear plastic wrap roll each half of the dough into a 12x8-inch rectangle. Peel off top sheet of wrap; invert dough onto a greased baking sheet; peel off remaining wrap. Cut dough into 2-inch squares. Bake crackers in a 350° oven for 18 to 20 minutes or till crisp and edges are golden. Remove and cool on wire racks. Store crackers in a tightly covered container. Makes 48 crackers.	

Jelly Jamboree

Sandwiches, muffins, toast, oatmeal . . . you name it. Kids will find all kinds of ways to empty a jar of jelly or jam. *You'll* feel much better about every sticky knifeful if you give them some not-so-sugary choices.

  Look for jelly and jam products at the grocery store that are labeled "low sugar," "all fruit," or "light." These spreads usually are made with less sugar than conventional jelly or jam, no sugar at all, or artificial sweeteners. Or, if you make your own jelly or jam, buy the fruit pectin that's labeled "light." It allows you to use one-third less sugar than standard pectins.

Whole Wheat Critters

2 cups whole wheat flour 1 cup all-purpose flour 1 teaspoon baking powder ½ cup margarine ½ cup packed brown sugar ⅓ cup honey 1 teaspoon vanilla	● In a large mixing bowl stir together flours and baking powder. Set aside. In a large mixer bowl beat margarine with an electric mixer on medium speed for 30 seconds. Add brown sugar, honey, and vanilla; beat till fluffy.
½ cup milk	● Add dry ingredients and milk alternately to beaten mixture, beating on low speed after each addition. Divide dough in half. Cover and chill several hours or till dough is easy to handle.
2 tablespoons sugar ½ teaspoon ground nutmeg	● On a lightly floured surface roll *half* of the dough ⅛ inch thick. Using large cookie cutters, cut into desired shapes; reroll as needed. 　Place on ungreased cookie sheets. Using tines of a fork, prick sparingly. Stir together sugar and nutmeg; sprinkle over dough. Repeat with remaining dough. 　Bake in a 350° oven about 10 minutes or till lightly browned around the edges. Remove and cool on wire racks. Makes about 36 cookies.

The kids will be reaching and the dog will be sniffing when you bake a batch of these crazy critters. The moms on our staff thought their kids would love to help cut out the dough.

Good-for-You Granola Bars

½ cup packed brown sugar ¼ cup margarine, melted ½ cup milk 1 egg	● In a mixing bowl combine sugar and margarine. Add milk and egg; mix well.
1½ cups Giddyap Granola (see recipe, page 12) *or* purchased granola ¾ cup whole wheat flour ½ teaspoon baking powder	● Stir together granola, flour, and baking powder. Stir into egg mixture. Spread batter into a greased and lightly floured 9x9x2-inch baking pan. 　Bake in a 350° oven for 20 to 25 minutes or till center is set. Cool in baking pan on a wire rack. Cut into bars. Makes 24 bars.

Any time is a good time for these scrumptious cereal bars. Grab one for a handy snack, a quick breakfast, or a satisfying dessert.

Vegetable Bouquets

2 tablespoons water 2 tablespoons vinegar 2 tablespoons cooking oil 1 teaspoon sugar ¼ teaspoon dried oregano, crushed Dash pepper	● For dressing, in a small bowl combine water, vinegar, oil, sugar, oregano, and pepper. Mix with a fork.
1 cup broccoli flowerets 1 cup cauliflower flowerets 1 medium carrot, cut into julienne strips	● In a large plastic bag set in a mixing bowl combine broccoli, cauliflower, and carrot. Pour dressing over vegetables. Cover and chill at least 2 hours, turning bag occasionally to coat vegetables.
	● To serve, drain vegetables and arrange in 4 miniature vases or 6-ounce custard cups to resemble bouquets. Serves 4.

What's better than getting a bouquet? Eating one! Especially if it's one of these broccoli, carrot, and cauliflower bouquets blooming with vitamins, minerals, and fiber.

Dreamy Dip

1½ cups low-fat cottage cheese 2 teaspoons lemon juice ½ cup plain low-fat yogurt	● In a blender container or food processor bowl combine cottage cheese and lemon juice. Cover and blend till very smooth. Add yogurt; blend well.
2 tablespoons snipped parsley 1 teaspoon dried dillweed 1 teaspoon dried minced onion Dash bottled hot pepper sauce (optional) Vegetable dippers	● In a mixing bowl stir together blended cottage cheese mixture, parsley, dillweed, minced onion, and hot pepper sauce, if desired. Serve with vegetable dippers. Cover and chill any remaining dip. Makes 1¾ cups.

There's more to this vegetable dip than meets the eye, because without the seasonings it's really a mock sour cream. So use it the same way you would real sour cream. You'll get only a fraction of the fat.

Party Shake

1 16-ounce can unsweetened applesauce, chilled
1 8-ounce carton vanilla low-fat yogurt
1 6-ounce can frozen apple juice concentrate
1 to 2 tablespoons sugar
10 ice cubes

● In a blender container combine all ingredients *except* ice. With blender running, add the ice cubes, one at a time, through opening in lid, blending till slushy. Transfer to glasses. Serves 10.

You don't need a party to try this fruity shake. But one sip is sure to make you want to celebrate.

Homemade Soda Pop

1 6-ounce can frozen lemonade concentrate, *or* orange, apple, grape, *or* pineapple juice concentrate, thawed
Carbonated water, chilled

● In a medium mixing bowl stir together fruit juice concentrate and 3 juice cans filled with carbonated water. (If using lemonade concentrate, increase carbonated water to 4 cans.) Gently stir till combined.

● Using a funnel, pour mixture into a 4-cup bottle or jar; seal. Chill up to 6 hours. Makes 4 (6-ounce) servings.

Most of our kid testers couldn't believe you could make soda pop at home. But one sip was all it took to convince even the staunchest cola lovers to switch to this fruity drink.
   Pssst, **moms and dads: The kids will love the flavor, but you'll love the fact that this drink is low in sugar and costs only pennies to make.**

Strawberry Smoothy

2 cups fresh *or* frozen unsweetened strawberries
1 12-ounce can lemon-lime carbonated beverage, chilled
Ice (optional)

● In a blender container combine strawberries and carbonated beverage. Cover and blend till smooth. Pour fruit mixture into 8-ounce glasses. Add ice, if desired. Makes 3 or 4 servings.

Use fresh berries and make a sippable drink, or try frozen berries and create a spoonable slush.

Nested Eggs

| 2 large potatoes | ● Peel and quarter potatoes. Cook potatoes, covered, in boiling water for 20 to 25 minutes or till tender. Drain. Mash with a potato masher or on low speed of an electric mixer. |

Some of the kids who spooned into this hearty egg casserole said they'd like it for breakfast.

| ¼ cup milk
½ cup shredded cheddar cheese (2 ounces)
¼ cup shredded carrot
¼ cup shredded zucchini
¼ teaspoon salt
⅛ teaspoon pepper | ● Add milk to mashed potatoes and mash till combined. Stir in cheddar cheese, carrot, zucchini, salt, and pepper. |

| 4 eggs | ● Spoon potato mixture into 4 lightly greased 10-ounce casseroles. With the back of a spoon, push potato mixture from center, building up sides. Carefully break *one* egg into the center of *each* casserole. Place casseroles on a baking sheet. Bake in a 425° oven about 15 minutes or till eggs are to desired doneness. Makes 4 servings. |

Chunky Chicken Bites

14 wheat crackers ¼ teaspoon ground sage ¼ teaspoon paprika	● Put wheat crackers, sage, and paprika in a plastic bag; close bag. Use a rolling pin to finely crush crackers. (You should have about ½ cup crumbs.)
2 whole medium chicken breasts, skinned, boned, and cut into 1-inch pieces 2 tablespoons milk	● In a small bowl dip chicken pieces into milk. Put chicken pieces in bag with crumbs. Close bag and shake to coat chicken. Place chicken in a single layer on a baking sheet or in a 15x10x1-inch baking pan. Bake in a 450° oven for 6 to 8 minutes or till chicken is no longer pink, turning pieces once.
Homemade Catsup (see recipe, page 72), purchased catsup, *or* bottled barbecue sauce	● To serve, dip chicken pieces into catsup or barbecue sauce. Serves 4.

The vote was overwhelming! These tender chunks of chicken were winners by a landslide. Most of the kid testers even campaigned for another serving.

Tick-Taco Chicken

1 2½- to 3-pound broiler-fryer chicken, cut up and skinned ½ cup fine dry bread crumbs 1 tablespoon nonfat dry milk powder 1½ teaspoons chili powder ¼ teaspoon garlic powder ¼ teaspoon dry mustard	● Rinse chicken; pat dry with paper towels. In a plastic bag combine bread crumbs, milk powder, chili powder, garlic powder, and mustard.
¼ cup milk	● Brush each chicken piece with milk. Place 2 or 3 pieces of chicken at a time in bag. Close bag and shake to coat.
	● Place chicken pieces, bone side down and so pieces don't touch, in a shallow baking pan. Sprinkle with any remaining crumb mixture. Bake in a 375° oven for 45 to 50 minutes or till chicken is no longer pink and coating is crisp. *Do not turn* chicken pieces. Makes 6 servings.

Instead of asking for seconds, kid tester Kristin asked for the recipe so her mom could make this chicken at home. Kristin can help by shaking the chicken in crumbs.

Vegetable-Garden Fish Fillets

1 **pound fresh *or* frozen cod *or* other fish fillets**
1 **7½-ounce can tomatoes, cut up**
1 **small zucchini, halved lengthwise and sliced**
1 **green pepper, cut into strips**
¼ **cup chopped onion**
½ **teaspoon dried thyme, crushed**
1 **clove garlic, minced**
1 **bay leaf**
Dash pepper
1 **tablespoon tomato paste**

● Thaw fish, if frozen. For sauce, in a skillet combine *undrained* tomatoes, zucchini, green pepper, onion, thyme, garlic, bay leaf, and pepper. Bring to boiling; reduce heat. Cover and simmer for 6 minutes. Uncover and simmer for 2 minutes more. Remove bay leaf; stir in tomato paste. Cover and keep warm.

This fish is more at home in the garden than in the ocean! The combination of fish and fresh vegetables will give you treasures of land and sea all in one catch.

Salt

● Sprinkle fish lightly with salt. Place fish in a greased skillet. Add water to cover. Bring to boiling; reduce heat. Cover and simmer 4 to 6 minutes per ½-inch thickness of fish or till fish flakes easily with a fork. Using a slotted spoon, transfer fish to serving plate. Spoon sauce over fish. Makes 4 servings.

Oven Orange Fish

1 **pound fresh *or* frozen fish fillets**
1 **slightly beaten egg**
1 **teaspoon finely shredded orange peel**
¼ **cup orange juice**

● Thaw fish, if frozen. In a shallow bowl combine egg, shredded orange peel, and orange juice.

The kids who tasted this baked fish couldn't tell that the crunchy topping was shredded wheat cereal. But they did know one thing: fish never tasted so good.

⅓ **cup crushed shredded wheat biscuit (1 large biscuit)**
Salt

● Dip fish fillets in egg mixture. Coat *one* side of each fillet with crushed shredded wheat. Place fish, crumb side up, in a 12x7½x2-inch baking dish. Sprinkle lightly with salt. Bake in a 500° oven for 10 to 15 minutes or till the fish flakes easily with a fork. Serves 4.

Deep-Sea Casserole

4 ounces medium shell macaroni *or* whole wheat spaghetti, broken into bite-size pieces

● Cook pasta according to package directions; drain.

Dive in! You'll get a mouthful of chunky tuna engulfed in a sea of pasta shells. What's more, this dish is lower in fat and sodium than most tuna casseroles.

1 cup sliced celery *or* chopped carrot
½ cup chopped onion
2 tablespoons margarine
¼ cup nonfat dry milk powder
2 tablespoons cornstarch
2 cups milk

● Meanwhile, for sauce, in a saucepan cook celery or carrot and onion in margarine till tender. Stir in dry milk powder and cornstarch. Add milk all at once. Cook and stir till thickened and bubbly. Cook and stir 2 minutes more.

1 9¼-ounce can tuna (water pack), drained and flaked
¼ cup snipped parsley
½ cup bite-size fish-shape crackers

● Carefully stir cooked pasta, tuna, and parsley into sauce. Transfer to a 1½-quart casserole. Bake, uncovered, in a 375° oven for 15 minutes. Arrange crackers on top. Bake about 5 minutes more or till heated through. Serves 6.

Microwave Method: Assemble casserole as directed above. Micro-cook, uncovered, on 100% power (high) for 3 to 4 minutes or till the mixture is heated through, stirring twice. Before serving, arrange crackers on top.

Mix-and-Match Multigrain Pizza

1 cup oat flour*
½ cup all-purpose flour
½ cup whole wheat flour
¼ cup yellow cornmeal
1 teaspoon baking powder
⅔ cup milk
¼ cup cooking oil

● Stir together oat flour, all-purpose flour, whole wheat flour, cornmeal, and baking powder. Add milk and oil; mix well. Knead gently on a lightly floured surface 10 to 12 strokes.

Press dough into a greased 12-inch pizza pan. Build up edges; cut at 1-inch intervals. Bake in a 425° oven for 12 to 15 minutes or till light brown.

Straight from the mouth of kid tester Alex: "Wow! This is great! I've never had pizza like this before." We bet you'll get a great reaction, too, if you let your kids customize their pizza with their favorite toppings.

½ pound lean ground beef, ground raw turkey, *or* ground turkey sausage
1 8-ounce can pizza sauce
2 cups torn spinach, romaine, *or* leaf lettuce
1 medium green pepper *or* zucchini, chopped, *or* 1 cup sliced fresh mushrooms
1½ cups shredded mozzarella, cheddar, *or* Monterey Jack cheese (6 ounces)

● Meanwhile, in a medium skillet cook meat till brown. Drain off fat, if necessary. Stir in pizza sauce. Arrange spinach, romaine, or lettuce on crust. Top with meat mixture. Arrange green pepper, zucchini, or mushrooms over meat mixture. Sprinkle with cheese.

● Return to the 425° oven for 10 to 15 minutes or till topping is heated through and cheese melts. Makes 6 servings.

*Note: For oat flour, in a blender container or food processor bowl place 1¼ cups regular or quick-cooking *rolled oats.* Cover and blend till fine.

Topsy-Turvy Pizza

1 **16-ounce package hot roll mix** 2 **tablespoons toasted wheat germ** 1 **cup frozen chopped broccoli *or* cauliflower** 1 **8-ounce can pizza sauce** ½ **teaspoon Italian seasoning, crushed** ⅛ **teaspoon pepper** 1½ **cups chopped cooked turkey *or* chicken (8 ounces)**	● Prepare hot roll mix according to package directions for pizza dough, *except* stir in the wheat germ. Let dough rest according to package directions. Meanwhile, cook broccoli or cauliflower in a small amount of lightly salted water about 2 minutes or till just crisp-tender; drain. In a medium saucepan combine pizza sauce, Italian seasoning, and pepper. Bring to boiling. Stir in turkey or chicken and vegetables.
2 **tablespoons grated Parmesan cheese** 1 **cup shredded mozzarella cheese (4 ounces)**	● Lightly grease the insides and outer rims of four 10- to 12-ounce baking dishes. Sprinkle Parmesan cheese on the bottoms of dishes. Divide mozzarella cheese evenly among the dishes. Spoon turkey-vegetable mixture into dishes.
Milk	● Divide dough into 8 portions. On a lightly floured suface roll or pat out each of the portions to extend ¾ inch beyond the edges of baking dishes. Using *four* of the portions, place *one* portion of dough on top of each dish. Brush with milk. Place remaining 4 portions of dough on a baking sheet. Freeze about 1 hour or till firm. Seal, label, and freeze for later use. To thaw, let dough stand at room temperature for 30 minutes or in the refrigerator for 1 hour.
	● Bake prepared pizzas in a 375° oven about 15 minutes or till dough is light brown. To serve, immediately loosen the crusts and invert pizzas onto serving plates. If necessary, carefully spread the filling to edges of crusts. Serves 4.

Who ever heard of upside-down pizza? It was a first for our kid testers, and they really flipped over the great flavor.

After each baking dish is filled with pizza filling, place dough on top of the dishes. Overlap the rims with the dough and press lightly to seal.

Hide-and-Seek Pizzas

1 **pound ground turkey sausage *or* lean ground beef**
1 **15-ounce can tomato sauce**
¼ **teaspoon garlic powder**

● In a medium skillet cook meat till brown. Drain off fat, if necessary. Stir in tomato sauce and garlic powder; cook and stir over low heat for 5 minutes. Remove from heat.

6 **large whole wheat pita bread rounds**
1 **cup shredded Monterey Jack *or* mozzarella cheese (4 ounces)**

● Using scissors or a knife, cut circles out of the tops of pita bread rounds. Remove tops. Place tops and bottoms on 2 baking sheets. Toast in a 450° oven for 3 to 4 minutes or till light brown. Spoon meat mixture into pita bread bottoms. Sprinkle with cheese.

● Place pita bottoms on a baking sheet. Bake in the 450° oven about 8 minutes or till hot. To serve, place pita bread tops over baked pizzas. Serves 6.

On the outside, these look like mild-mannered pita bread rounds. But lift off the tops to reveal super meal-in-one pizzas.

Using scissors or a sharp knife, cut circles out of the tops of the pita bread, leaving about 1-inch rims. Remove top portions.

Ham-It-Up Salad

1 **8-ounce can pineapple chunks (juice pack)**

● Drain pineapple, reserving juice. Set pineapple aside.

1 **cup low-fat cottage cheese**
1 **tablespoon lemon juice**
1 **small apple, cored and chopped**
1 **teaspoon poppy seed**

● For dressing, in a blender container or food processor bowl combine cottage cheese, lemon juice, and reserved pineapple juice. Cover and blend till smooth. Stir in chopped apple and poppy seed. Cover and chill.

1½ **cups fully cooked ham cut into julienne strips**
1 **cup seedless red *or* green grapes, halved**
½ **cup sliced celery**
2 **ounces mozzarella cheese, cut into julienne strips (½ cup)**
5 **cups torn lettuce**

● In a medium mixing bowl combine ham, grapes, celery, mozzarella cheese, and reserved pineapple. Cover and chill. Before serving, toss ham mixture with lettuce. Spoon on dressing; toss to coat. Makes 6 to 8 servings.

Nothing can disguise the terrific flavor of this main-dish salad. And it's easy enough for your pint-size practical joker to prepare.

Macaroni Cloud in a Mug

2 ounces whole wheat elbow macaroni (½ cup) 2 tablespoons finely chopped green pepper 1 tablespoon finely chopped onion	● In a medium saucepan cook macaroni, uncovered, in boiling salted water for 6 minutes. Add green pepper and onion and cook for 2 minutes more. Drain in a colander. Rinse with cold water; drain again.
1 cup milk 4 teaspoons cornstarch ¼ teaspoon salt Dash pepper Dash bottled hot pepper sauce 1½ cups shredded cheddar cheese (6 ounces) 1 cup frozen whole kernel corn, thawed	● In the same saucepan stir together milk and cornstarch. Stir in salt, pepper, and hot pepper sauce. Cook and stir till thickened and bubbly. Reduce heat to low. Add cheese and corn, stirring till cheese melts. Remove from heat.
2 egg yolks 2 egg whites ⅛ teaspoon cream of tartar	● In a medium mixing bowl lightly beat egg yolks with a wire wisk or fork. Slowly add cheese mixture, stirring constantly. Fold in macaroni mixture; cool slightly. In a small mixer bowl beat egg whites and cream of tartar till stiff peaks form (tips stand straight). Fold into cheese-macaroni mixture.
	● Fill four 12-ounce ovenproof mugs or 10-ounce custard cups with the egg mixture, leaving a ¼-inch headspace in each. Place on a baking sheet or shallow baking pan. Bake in a 325° oven for 30 to 35 minutes or till the tops are golden brown and a knife inserted near the centers comes out clean. Serves 4.

You'll be floating on cloud nine when you spoon into this heavenly macaroni and cheese. If you don't have mugs that are ovenproof, use 10-ounce custard cups instead.

Garden-Patch Macaroni

1 cup mixed spinach and carrot corkscrew *or* elbow macaroni	● Cook macaroni according to package directions; drain.
2 tablespoons margarine 2 tablespoons all-purpose flour Dash pepper 1 cup milk 1 cup cubed American cheese (4 ounces)	● Meanwhile, for sauce, in a medium saucepan melt margarine. Stir in flour and pepper; add milk all at once. Cook and stir till thickened and bubbly. Add cheese; stir till cheese melts.
1 cup frozen peas, whole kernel corn, *or* cut green beans 1 medium tomato, sliced (optional)	● Stir together cooked pasta, sauce, and frozen vegetables. Transfer mixture to a 1-quart casserole. Bake, uncovered, in a 350° oven for 20 to 25 minutes or till heated through. If desired, arrange tomato on top and bake about 5 minutes more or till tomato is warm. Makes 4 servings.

Chili Macaroni: Prepare Garden-Patch Macaroni as directed above, *except* stir 1 teaspoon *chili powder* into the melted margarine with the flour and pepper. Stir one 8-ounce can drained *red kidney beans* into sauce with the cooked pasta. Omit frozen vegetables.

This healthful version of macaroni and cheese is a good way to get kids to eat their vegetables. Each cheesy bite contains spinach and carrot pasta and peas, corn, or beans.

Mexican Spaghetti Pie

6 ounces whole wheat,
 spinach, *or* regular
 spaghetti
2 beaten eggs
¼ cup grated Parmesan
 cheese

● Cook spaghetti according to package directions; drain. Stir in eggs and Parmesan cheese. Spread spaghetti mixture in a greased 12-inch pizza pan.

Silencio! That's exactly what we got when our kid testers tasted this special pie. They were too busy eating to talk!

¾ pound lean ground beef
1 small onion, chopped
1 8-ounce can tomato sauce
1 teaspoon chili powder

● In a skillet cook beef and onion till meat is brown and onion is tender. Drain off fat. Stir in tomato sauce and chili powder. Bring to boiling; reduce heat. Cover and simmer for 5 minutes.

2 medium tomatoes,
 chopped
½ cup shredded cheddar
 cheese (2 ounces)
1 cup shredded lettuce

● Spoon meat mixture over spaghetti mixture to within 1 inch of edge. Bake, uncovered, in a 350° oven for 10 minutes. Top with tomatoes; sprinkle with cheese. Bake for 4 to 5 minutes more or till cheese melts. Top with lettuce. Cut into wedges. Serves 6.

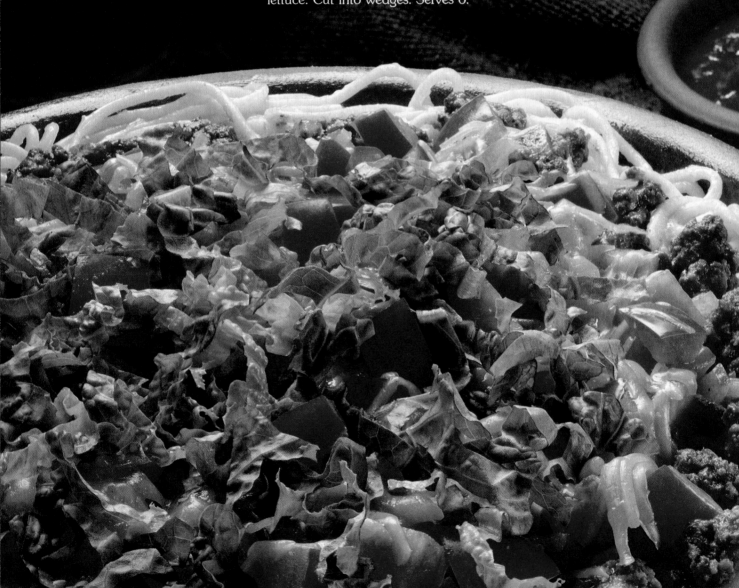

Enchilada Cones
(See recipe, page 52)

Enchilada Cones

Pictured on page 51.

6 **6-inch corn tortillas**
¼ **cup chopped onion**
¼ **cup water**
½ **teaspoon instant chicken bouillon granules**

● Wrap tortillas in foil and heat in a 350° oven about 10 minutes or till warm. Meanwhile, in a small saucepan combine onion, water, and bouillon granules. Bring to boiling; reduce heat. Cover and simmer about 1 minute or till onion is tender. *Do not drain.*

These tortilla cones are stuffed with a cheesy chicken filling and topped with a mild homemade salsa. The cone shape makes them easy for kids to pick up and eat with their hands.

1 **3-ounce package cream cheese, cut up**
2 **cups diced cooked chicken *or* turkey**
2 **tablespoons snipped parsley**

● Stir cream cheese into onion mixture in saucepan till smooth. Stir in chicken or turkey and parsley.

½ **cup shredded Monterey Jack cheese (2 ounces)**

● Unwrap tortillas. For each tortilla, make 1 cut from center of tortilla to the outside edge. Place in a 6-ounce custard cup, overlapping sides. Sprinkle cheese into bottom of each tortilla cone. Spoon chicken mixture into each tortilla cone on top of cheese. Place custard cups on a baking sheet. Bake in a 350° oven for 20 to 25 minutes or till heated through.

1 **8-ounce can tomato sauce**
½ **of a 4-ounce can diced green chili peppers, drained**
1 **teaspoon sugar**
¼ **teaspoon ground coriander (optional)**

● Meanwhile, for sauce, in a saucepan combine tomato sauce, green chili peppers, sugar, and coriander, if desired. Cook and stir till heated through. Transfer tortilla cones to dinner plates. Serve with sauce. Makes 6 servings.

To shape a tortilla into a cone, make one cut in a tortilla from the center to the edge. Place the tortilla in a custard cup, overlapping the cut sides to form a cone shape.

Jogger Joes

1 pound lean ground beef *or* ground raw turkey 1 medium onion, chopped 1 cup tomato juice 1 8-ounce can tomato sauce 2 teaspoons prepared mustard 1 teaspoon chili powder 1 teaspoon Worcestershire sauce	● In a large skillet cook meat and onion till meat is brown and onion is tender. Drain off fat. Stir in tomato juice, tomato sauce, mustard, chili powder, and Worcestershire sauce.	For Jordan and LaToya, two of our kid testers, cleaning their plates was a race to the finish. One meaty sandwich wasn't enough, though; they asked for doggy bags and each took one home!
¾ cup bite-size wheat square cereal, slightly crushed 6 whole wheat hamburger buns, split	● Stir crushed cereal into meat mixture in skillet. Bring to boiling; reduce heat. Simmer, uncovered, for 10 minutes, stirring occasionally. Spoon meat mixture into buns. Makes 6 servings.	A sneaky way to add fiber and thicken the lean meat mixture is with crushed whole wheat cereal.

Small-Fry Stir-Fry

⅓ cup water 2 tablespoons soy sauce 2 teaspoons cornstarch ⅛ teaspoon garlic powder ⅛ teaspoon ground ginger ⅛ teaspoon pepper	● For sauce, in a small bowl stir together water, soy sauce, cornstarch, garlic powder, ground ginger, and pepper; set aside.	The small fry loved this stir-fry and wanted to know more about the rice it was served with. Brown rice is unpolished; its outer hull and a small portion of its bran are removed (for white rice, processors remove all of the bran).
1 tablespoon cooking oil 1½ cups thinly sliced carrots *or* cauliflower 1 cup fresh pea pods *or* one 6-ounce package frozen pea pods, thawed 1 cup bean sprouts	● Preheat a wok or 12-inch skillet over high heat; add cooking oil. (Add more oil as necessary during cooking.) Add carrots or cauliflower; stir-fry over high heat for 3 minutes. Add pea pods and bean sprouts; stir-fry for 1 minute more. Remove vegetables from wok.	Brown rice is chewier than white rice and takes longer to cook. To get 2 cups cooked brown rice, start with ⅔ cup uncooked rice. Add the rice to 1⅓ cups boiling water. Cover and simmer for 30 to 40 minutes.
¾ pound lean ground beef 2 cups hot cooked brown rice	● Add beef to wok. Stir-fry about 3 minutes or till meat is brown. Thoroughly drain off fat. Push meat from center of wok. Stir sauce; add to center of wok. Cook and stir till thickened and bubbly. Cook and stir 1 minute more. Return stir-fried vegetables to wok; stir all ingredients together to coat with sauce. Cook and stir for 1 minute more. Serve over rice. Makes 4 servings.	

Nuts-About-Fruit Salad

1 **8-ounce can crushed pineapple (juice pack)**
1 **cup shredded carrot**
1 **cup chopped apple *or* pear**
½ **cup peanuts**
¼ **cup raisins *or* chopped pitted dates**

● Drain pineapple; reserve *1 tablespoon* juice. In a mixing bowl combine pineapple, carrot, apple or pear, peanuts, and raisins or dates.

⅓ **cup plain low-fat yogurt**
2 **tablespoons peanut butter**
Leaf lettuce

● Combine yogurt and peanut butter till smooth. Stir in reserved pineapple juice; stir into fruit mixture. Cover and chill. Serve in a lettuce-lined bowl. Serves 6.

Jumble Salad

¾ cup low-fat cottage
    cheese, drained
¼ cup lemon low-fat yogurt
½ cup seedless red *or* green
    grapes, halved
¼ cup canned crushed
    pineapple (juice pack),
    drained
¼ cup sliced celery

● In a small bowl combine cottage cheese and lemon yogurt. Stir in grapes, pineapple, and celery. Cover and chill.

Toss together cottage cheese, yogurt, grapes, pineapple, and celery. You'll get a hodgepodge of flavors in this cool and calcium-packed salad.

    Shredded lettuce
2 tablespoons chopped
    walnuts (optional)

● To serve, arrange lettuce on 4 salad plates. Spoon cottage cheese mixture onto lettuce; sprinkle with chopped walnuts, if desired. Serves 4.

Sprout 'n' Spud Salad

3 medium potatoes

● Scrub potatoes. In a medium saucepan cook unpeeled potatoes, covered, in boiling water for 25 to 30 minutes or till tender; drain. Cool potatoes slightly; cube.

Whether you call it a potato or spud, this versatile vegetable is loaded with vitamin C, vitamin B$_6$, potassium, and iron.

¼ cup plain low-fat yogurt
¼ cup mayonnaise *or* salad
    dressing
2 tablespoons snipped
    parsley
1 tablespoon sliced green
    onion
2 teaspoons snipped fresh
    basil *or* ½ teaspoon
    dried basil, crushed
½ cup frozen peas
½ cup bean sprouts,
    chopped

● In a medium mixing bowl combine yogurt, mayonnaise or salad dressing, parsley, green onion, and basil. Add potatoes, frozen peas, and bean sprouts; stir lightly to coat. Cover and chill several hours. Makes 4 or 5 servings.

Rocket Ship Salad

1 large banana
  Lemon juice
2 slices pineapple
⅔ cup low-fat cottage cheese

● Peel banana; cut in half crosswise and lengthwise. Brush with lemon juice. Place each banana quarter with long flat side down on a plate. Cut pineapple slices into quarters. Place 2 pineapple quarters near the base of each banana quarter. Spoon cottage cheese around bottom to resemble exhaust. Makes 4 servings.

3, 2, 1 . . . Blast off with this easy-on-the-chef fruit salad. It caused explosive excitement among our kid testers.

Mamma Mia Zucchini

1 7½-ounce can tomatoes, cut up	● Reserve *1 tablespoon* tomato juice from tomatoes; set aside.	**Close your eyes and imagine you're in Venice. Now you're ready to dig into this combination of Italian seasoning, vegetables, and grated Parmesan cheese.**
1 cup frozen *or* one 8-ounce can whole kernel corn, drained ¼ teaspoon Italian seasoning, crushed Dash onion powder 1 medium zucchini, quartered lengthwise and sliced ¼ inch thick	● In a 1-quart saucepan combine *undrained* tomatoes, corn, Italian seasoning, and onion powder. Bring to boiling; reduce heat. Cover and simmer for 2 minutes. Stir in zucchini. Cook, uncovered, about 3 minutes more or till zucchini is just tender.	
1 teaspoon cornstarch Grated Parmesan cheese	● Stir together the reserved tomato juice and cornstarch. Stir into vegetable mixture. Cook and stir till thickened and bubbly. Cook and stir 2 minutes more. Sprinkle with Parmesan cheese. Serves 4.	

Microwave Method: Reserve *1 tablespoon* tomato juice from tomatoes; set aside. In a 1-quart microwave-safe casserole combine *undrained* tomatoes, corn, Italian seasoning and onion powder. Micro-cook, covered, on 100% power (high) for 3 minutes. Stir in zucchini. Cook, covered, 3 to 4 minutes more or till just tender, stirring once.

Stir together reserved tomato juice and cornstarch. Stir into vegetable mixture. Cook, uncovered, for 1 to 2 minutes more or till thickened and bubbly, stirring every 30 seconds. Sprinkle with Parmesan cheese.

Riceghetti Pilaf

3 ounces spaghetti *or* linguine, broken into 1-inch pieces (about ½ cup) 1 teaspoon cooking oil ½ cup uncooked brown rice 1 14½-ounce can chicken broth ¼ cup water 1 tablespoon snipped parsley	● In a medium saucepan cook spaghetti or linguine in hot oil till light brown. Remove from heat. Stir in rice. Carefully add chicken broth and water. Bring to boiling; reduce heat. Cover and simmer about 40 minutes or till liquid is absorbed. (Rice will be slightly chewy.) Stir in parsley. Makes 4 servings.	**Please both the pasta lovers and rice lovers by serving this doubly delicious side dish.**

Chow-Down Chowder

1 14½-ounce can chicken broth
1 cup frozen cut broccoli *or* green beans

● In a small saucepan bring broth and broccoli or green beans to boiling. Reduce heat; cover and simmer for 5 minutes. *Do not drain.* Set aside.

The name fits! Our kid testers downed this hearty vegetable soup spoonful after spoonful.

1 cup sliced fresh mushrooms
½ cup chopped onion
1 tablespoon margarine
2 tablespoons all-purpose flour
¼ teaspoon salt
⅛ teaspoon pepper
1 13-ounce can (1⅔ cups) evaporated skim milk
1 8-ounce can whole kernel corn, drained
1 tablespoon chopped pimiento
Crackers (optional)

● In a large saucepan cook mushrooms and onion in margarine till tender. Stir in flour, salt, and pepper. Add milk all at once. Cook and stir till thickened and bubbly. Cook and stir 1 minute more. Stir in broccoli or beans with broth, corn, and pimiento; heat through. Serve with crackers, if desired. Makes 6 servings.

Creamy Potato Soup

4	cups chicken broth
1	medium carrot, sliced
1	stalk celery, sliced
½	teaspoon dried dillweed
	Dash pepper

● In a large saucepan combine chicken broth, carrot, celery, dillweed, and pepper. Bring to boiling; reduce heat. Cover and simmer for 10 minutes.

Put away the peeler. You'll get more fiber and vitamins if you leave the skins on the potatoes when you make this hearty soup.

| 3 | cups cubed potatoes (1¼ pounds) |

● Add potatoes to saucepan. Cover and cook about 15 minutes or till potatoes are tender.

| ¾ | cup milk |
| 3 | tablespoons all-purpose flour |

● Stir together milk and flour. Add to mixture in saucepan. Cook and stir till thickened and bubbly. Cook and stir 1 minute more. Makes 5 servings.

Mixed-Grain Corn Bread

1⅓	cups yellow cornmeal
¾	cup whole wheat flour
¼	cup toasted wheat germ
2	tablespoons sesame seed
2½	teaspoons baking powder
½	teaspoon baking soda
¼	teaspoon salt

● In a medium mixing bowl stir together cornmeal, whole wheat flour, wheat germ, sesame seed, baking powder, baking soda, and salt.

The kid testers couldn't agree whether to spread butter, honey butter, honey, or nothing at all on this tender bread. But they all spread the word that it tastes great.

1	egg
¼	cup cooking oil
2	cups buttermilk

● Beat together egg and cooking oil; add buttermilk. Stir buttermilk mixture into dry ingredients till moistened (do not overstir). Pour into a greased 9x9x2-inch baking pan. Bake in a 400° oven about 25 minutes or till golden brown. Serve warm. Makes 8 to 10 servings.

Bottoms-Up Carrot Cake

1 8-ounce can pineapple slices (juice pack) **1 tablespoon margarine** **2 tablespoons brown sugar**	● Drain pineapple, reserving juice. Halve pineapple slices. Melt margarine in a 9x1½-inch round baking pan. Stir in brown sugar and *1 tablespoon* reserved pineapple juice. Arrange pineapple in pan; set aside.	**Flipping this cake over really gets to the bottom of things; namely, the gooey pineapple topping that makes a great stand-in for frosting.**
1 cup whole wheat flour **½ cup packed brown sugar** **½ teaspoon baking powder** **½ teaspoon baking soda** **½ teaspoon ground cinnamon** **1½ cups finely shredded carrot** **⅓ cup cooking oil** **2 eggs**	● In a large mixer bowl stir together flour, brown sugar, baking powder, baking soda, and cinnamon. Add carrot, oil, and eggs to dry ingredients. Beat with an electric mixer on medium speed till combined. Continue beating on medium speed for 2 minutes more.	
	● Gently spoon batter evenly into pan over pineapple mixture. Bake in a 325° oven about 35 minutes or till a wooden toothpick inserted near the center comes out clean. Cool 5 minutes in pan. Invert onto a serving plate. Serve warm. Makes 8 to 10 servings.	**To reheat 1 serving of the cake, place on a microwave-safe plate. Micro-cook, uncovered, on 100% power (high) for 20 to 30 seconds.**

Sherlock's Cake

1½ cups all-purpose flour
1 cup whole wheat flour
½ cup unsweetened cocoa powder
2½ teaspoons baking powder
½ teaspoon baking soda

● Grease and lightly flour a 13x9x2-inch baking pan or 10-inch tube pan. Stir together flours, cocoa powder, baking powder, and baking soda.

¾ cup margarine
1½ cups packed brown sugar
3 eggs
2 teaspoons vanilla

● In a large mixer bowl beat margarine on medium speed of electric mixer for 30 seconds. Add sugar and beat till fluffy. Add eggs, one at a time, beating well on medium speed. Beat in vanilla.

½ cup milk
1½ cups finely shredded unpeeled zucchini (2 medium)
1 cup chopped walnuts
Powdered sugar

● Add dry ingredients and milk alternately to beaten mixture, beating on low speed after each addition. Stir in zucchini and nuts. Spread batter evenly into prepared pan.
  Bake in a 350° oven for 30 to 35 minutes for the 13x9x2-inch cake, or 1¼ hours for the 10-inch tube cake, or till a wooden toothpick inserted near the center comes out clean. (If using a 10-inch tube pan, cool cake in pan on a wire rack for 10 minutes. Remove cake from pan and cool thoroughly.) Sift powdered sugar over cake. Serves 24.

Shhh! Don't breathe a word about the zucchini, because not even a magnifying glass could give away the clue to this luscious chocolate cake. Now your kids can have their cake and eat their vegetables, too.

Fruity Mash

1 ripe small banana,
⅔ cup sliced fresh
strawberries, *or* 1 small
peach *or* apricot,
peeled and sliced
½ cup vanilla low-fat yogurt
⅛ teaspoon ground nutmeg

● In a small mixing bowl mash fruit. Stir in yogurt and nutmeg. Makes 2 servings.

Just do what the title says: Mash some fruit, then combine it with vanilla yogurt and nutmeg. This tastes so good your kids won't even know they're eating a calcium-packed dessert that's low in sugar and fat.

Apple Volcanoes

1 large cooking apple,
peeled
1 cup boiling water
3 tablespoons peanut butter

● Core apple. Cut crosswise into 6 slices. In a 10-inch skillet cook apple slices, covered, in boiling water for 3 to 5 minutes or till crisp-tender. Remove from skillet and drain on paper towels. Spread about *½ tablespoon* peanut butter on *each* slice of apple. Place in a shallow baking pan, peanut butter side up.

Paul, one of our kid testers, came up with this imaginative title. He thought the peanut butter looked like lava and the baked meringue topping like smoke.

2 egg whites
¼ teaspoon ground
cinnamon
2 tablespoons sugar

● In a small mixer bowl beat egg whites and cinnamon with an electric mixer on medium speed till soft peaks form (tips curl). Gradually add sugar, beating on high speed till stiff peaks form (tips stand straight).

● Spoon egg-white mixture over apple slices, making peaks in the egg-white mixture. Bake in a 400° oven for 8 to 10 minutes or till topping is light brown. Serve warm. Makes 6 servings.

To assemble the dessert, spoon the beaten egg-white mixture over the apple slices. Use the back of the spoon to make peaks in the egg-white mixture.

Fruit Baskets

2 large shredded wheat biscuits **¼ cup coconut** **1 tablespoon brown sugar** **¼ cup margarine, melted**	● Crumble shredded wheat biscuits; stir in coconut and sugar. Drizzle with melted margarine; toss to coat.
	● Line six 6-ounce custard cups or muffin cups with foil. Press mixture onto the bottoms and up the sides of lined cups. Bake in a 350° oven about 10 minutes or till crisp. Cool in cups. Remove from cups by lifting foil. Peel foil off baskets.
Fresh fruit (apples, bananas, pears, berries, plums, peaches, *or* melon) **Vanilla low-fat yogurt** **Ground nutmeg *or* cinnamon (optional)**	● Cut up fruit, if necessary. Fill baskets with fruit. Top with vanilla yogurt and sprinkle with nutmeg or cinnamon, if desired. Makes 6 servings.

You might be tempted to use these baskets of goodies as centerpieces. Although they're nice to look at, they're even better to eat.

Branana Bars

½ cup all-purpose flour **½ cup whole wheat flour** **¼ cup unprocessed wheat bran** **1 teaspoon baking powder** **⅛ teaspoon salt** **⅛ teaspoon ground allspice**	● In a medium mixing bowl stir together all-purpose flour, whole wheat flour, bran, baking powder, salt, and allspice.
1 beaten egg **⅓ cup packed brown sugar** **¼ cup cooking oil** **¼ cup milk** **½ teaspoon vanilla** **1 ripe medium banana, mashed (⅓ cup)** **⅓ cup mixed dried fruit bits *or* raisins**	● In a large mixing bowl stir together egg, brown sugar, oil, milk, and vanilla. Add banana and fruit bits or raisins; stir till combined. Stir dry ingredients into banana mixture. Spread batter evenly in a greased 11x7x1½-inch baking pan. Bake in a 350° oven for 20 to 25 minutes or till a wooden toothpick inserted near the center comes out clean. Cool in pan on a wire rack. Cut into bars.
3 tablespoons sifted powdered sugar **¼ teaspoon vanilla** **1 to 1¼ teaspoons milk**	● For frosting, stir together powdered sugar and vanilla. Add enough milk to make of drizzling consistency. Drizzle over bars. Makes 16 bars.

One taste was worth a thousand words. All of the kids who tasted these wholesome bar cookies finished every last morsel. Need we say more?

Playful-Dough Pizza Cookie

⅔ cup margarine ⅓ cup sugar ½ teaspoon almond *or* vanilla extract Food coloring (optional)	● In a large mixer bowl beat margarine with an electric mixer on medium speed about 30 seconds or till softened. Add sugar, almond or vanilla extract, and food coloring, if desired. Beat till fluffy.
1 cup whole wheat flour ⅔ cup all-purpose flour	● With mixer on low speed, gradually add flours, beating till mixture resembles coarse crumbs. Form dough into a ball.
	● Press dough into an ungreased 12-inch pizza pan. Bake in a 300° oven for 25 to 30 minutes or till edge of dough is firm. Cool.

1 8-ounce container
    reduced-calorie
    soft-style cream cheese
2 tablespoons milk
1 teaspoon finely shredded
    orange *or* lemon peel
	● Meanwhile, in a small mixing bowl stir together cream cheese, milk, and orange or lemon peel.

Desired fruit
    (sliced strawberries,
    apples, kiwi fruit, *or*
    bananas; mandarin
    orange sections; *or*
    halved seedless grapes)
Coconut (optional)
	● Spread cream cheese mixture over baked crust. Top with fruit. Sprinkle with coconut, if desired. Cut into wedges. Makes 10 to 12 servings.

Make the cookie crust any color you want by adding about ¼ teaspoon food coloring to the dough.

Monkey Crisp

3 medium bananas Lemon juice Ground cinnamon	● Cut bananas into ¼-inch slices. Arrange slices in a 9-inch pie plate. Brush banana slices with lemon juice; sprinkle lightly with cinnamon.
3 tablespoons whole wheat flour 3 tablespoons quick-cooking rolled oats 2 tablespoons brown sugar 2 tablespoons chopped peanuts 2 tablespoons margarine	● In a small mixing bowl stir together flour, rolled oats, brown sugar, and peanuts. With a fork, cut in margarine till mixture resembles crumbs. Sprinkle crumb mixture over bananas.
	● Bake in a 400° oven for 12 to 15 minutes or till bananas are heated through. Serve warm. Serves 4 or 5.

Here's a new twist on apple crisp. Use bananas for the apples and sprinkle with a nutty whole grain topper.

Applicious Granola Crunch

1 20-ounce can sliced apples ½ teaspoon ground cinnamon	● In a medium saucepan combine *undrained* apples and cinnamon. Stir gently over medium heat till hot.
6 ½-cup scoops vanilla ice milk ¾ cup Giddyap Granola (see recipe, page 12) *or* purchased granola	● Place ice milk in individual bowls. Spoon warm apple mixture over ice milk; sprinkle with granola. Serves 6.

Question: What do you call a delicious and nutritious ice-cream sundae made with apples?

Answer: APPLICIOUS! Hot apple slices and granola replace the traditional hot fudge and nuts in this cool and creamy indulgence.

Peanut-Bran Drops

1½	cups whole bran cereal
¾	cup all-purpose flour
½	cup whole wheat flour
1	teaspoon baking powder
½	teaspoon baking soda

● In a medium mixing bowl stir together whole bran cereal, all-purpose flour, whole wheat flour, baking powder, and baking soda.

We sneaked a fistful of fiber into these crunchy cookies by using whole wheat flour, bran cereal, and nuts.

¾	cup margarine
¾	cup packed brown sugar
1	egg
1	teaspoon vanilla
¾	cup chopped peanuts

● In a large mixer bowl beat margarine and sugar till fluffy. Add egg and vanilla; beat well. Add dry ingredients; beat till well combined. Stir in peanuts.

● Drop dough by rounded teaspoons 2 inches apart onto an ungreased cookie sheet. Bake in a 350° oven for 10 to 12 minutes or till done. Remove and cool on wire racks. Makes about 36 cookies.

How Sweet It Is

The next time your little one's sweet tooth demands attention, give it some. As long as you're careful about what kinds of desserts you serve, you can satisfy that craving without sabotaging good eating.

Try nature's candy, fruit, for a grand finale. Serve cut up fresh or unsweetened frozen fruits, or canned fruits packed in water or their own juice. Or try one of the recipes in this chapter for a sensibly sweet ending to any meal.

If it's ice cream they're screaming for, take a good look in your grocer's freezer case. Instead of grabbing a high-fat ice cream, pick up a carton of ice milk, which contains from 2 to 7 percent milk fat (ice cream has at least 10 percent milk fat). And don't forget one of the newest additions to the freezer section, frozen fruit and juice bars. They come in a variety of flavors to please even the pickiest licker.

Sprouts!

It's fun and easy to grow your own sprouts. Not only do they taste good, but each sprouted bean or seed is a miniature storehouse of nutrients. Sprouts contain vitamins and minerals, they're low in calories, and they're easier to digest than the beans themselves.

● When buying beans or seeds to sprout, make sure you get them at a supermarket or health food store. Never use beans or seeds that are sold for gardening. They are treated with fungicides that are poisonous.

● You don't need any special equipment to grow sprouts and you can start them any time of year. Use them in salads, soups, sandwiches, breads, casseroles, dips, and spreads.

● Store sprouts in a covered container in the refrigerator. They're best if eaten within a few days but will keep about one week. You can also freeze sprouts, but they will lose their crispness when thawed.

Sprout Gardening In a Jar

This method of sprouting is recommended for beans and some grains (see chart, page 70). Wash and sort beans, discarding damaged ones. Cover beans with water. Let beans stand at room temperature overnight. Drain and rinse beans.

Place beans in a clean glass jar (allow about ¼ cup soaked beans per 1-quart jar). Cover top of jar with a plastic perforated lid (sold in sprouting kits) or 2 layers of cheesecloth. Screw on lid or fasten cheesecloth with rubber band.

Place jar on its side so beans form a shallow layer. Store in a warm (65° to 75°), dark place. Rinse beans daily by pouring water into jar, swirling water around, and pouring it out through holes in lid or cheesecloth. Make sure you drain the beans thoroughly. Remove any moldy beans, if necessary.

Sprouts are usually ready to eat in 3 to 5 days. If desired, place sprouts in a bowl, cover with water, and stir to remove hulls. Skim away hulls as they rise to the top. Drain. Pat sprouts dry with paper towels.

Sprout Gardening On a Tray

This method of sprouting is recommended for most seeds (see chart, page 70). Cover the seeds with water. Let stand at room temperature about 3 hours or till seeds swell. Drain seeds. Line a shallow tray with 3 layers of paper towels; top with a single layer of cheesecloth. Arrange seeds in a single layer over cheesecloth. Spray thoroughly with a fine water spray. (Paper towels should be wet, but seeds shouldn't stand in water.)

Tear off a piece of foil large enough to cover tray; prick holes in foil. Cover tray loosely with the foil. Store in a warm (65° to 75°), dark place. Uncover tray and spray with water 4 or 5 times a day until seeds sprout and grow ¼ inch. Then spray 2 or 3 times a day, keeping sprouts moist at all times.

Sprouts are usually ready to eat in 3 to 5 days. At that time, remove foil and set tray in a sunny place for several hours to let the leaves turn green. Continue spraying sprouts. To harvest the sprouts, pull them off of the cheesecloth.

	BEAN OR SEED	YIELD	METHOD	FLAVOR/ TEXTURE
	Alfalfa seed	2 tablespoons alfalfa seed = 4 cups sprouts	Jar or tray	Mild/tender
	Barley	2 tablespoons barley = 1 cup sprouts	Jar	Mild/crunchy
	Buckwheat groats	¼ cup buckwheat groats = 2 cups sprouts	Jar or tray	Nutty/tender
	Lentils	2 tablespoons lentils = 1½ cups sprouts	Jar or tray	Mild/crisp
	Mung beans	¼ cup mung beans = 1½ cups sprouts	Jar	Mild/crunchy
	Radish seed	2 tablespoons radish seed = 1 cup sprouts	Tray	Peppery/tender
	Rye berries	¼ cup rye berries = 1 cup sprouts	Jar	Slightly sweet/tender
	Wheat berries	¼ cup wheat berries = 1 cup sprouts	Jar	Sweet and nutty/tender

Homemade Peanut Butter

1½ **cups unsalted dry roasted peanuts**
¼ **teaspoon salt**

● Place peanuts and salt in a blender container or food processor bowl. Cover and blend or process till spreadable. (This will take 6 to 7 minutes.) Stop and scrape sides of blender or food processor as necessary. Cover and chill peanut butter at least 1 hour before serving. Store in a covered container up to several months in the refrigerator. Makes about ¾ cup peanut butter.

Chunk-Style Peanut Butter: Prepare Homemade Peanut Butter as directed above, *except* stir an extra ½ cup chopped unsalted dry roasted *peanuts* into the blended mixture. Makes about 1 cup peanut butter.

Cinnamon Peanut Butter: Prepare Homemade Peanut Butter or Chunk-Style Peanut Butter as directed above, *except* add ¾ teaspoon ground *cinnamon* to blender container or food processor bowl with peanuts and salt. Makes ¾ to 1 cup peanut butter.

Not only is peanut butter fun and easy to make at home, it's also good for you. Our version of this kid-favorite food is low in salt and free of additives and preservatives.

Homemade Catsup

2 cups water
1 small onion, chopped
½ cup vinegar
3 tablespoons sugar
1 teaspoon dry mustard
½ teaspoon salt
¼ teaspoon celery seed
⅛ teaspoon ground
   cinnamon
⅛ teaspoon ground cloves
⅛ teaspoon dried basil,
   crushed
⅛ teaspoon ground cumin
⅛ teaspoon pepper
1 clove garlic, quartered

● In a blender container or food processor bowl combine *1 cup* water, onion, vinegar, sugar, mustard, salt, celery seed, cinnamon, cloves, basil, cumin, pepper, and garlic. Cover and blend or process till smooth.

This full-flavored, low-salt catsup is easy to freeze. Simply cool the cooked catsup slightly and pour into freezer containers, leaving a ½-inch head-space in each container. Cool catsup completely, then seal, label, and freeze. Store up to 10 months in the freezer.

1 12-ounce can tomato
   paste

● Pour mixture into a large saucepan. Stir in remaining water. Bring to boiling; reduce heat. Simmer, uncovered, for 20 minutes. Stir in tomato paste with a wire whisk. Simmer, uncovered, for 5 to 10 minutes more or to desired consistency (mixture may spatter). Pour into jars. Cover and store in the refrigerator up to 1 month. Makes about 2 cups.

Homemade Yogurt

2 cups milk **3 tablespoons nonfat dry milk powder**	● In a saucepan combine milk and nonfat dry milk powder. Heat to 120°.
2 tablespoons plain low-fat yogurt	● Place yogurt in a mixing bowl; stir in warm milk mixture. Cover bowl with plastic wrap and a towel. Place in a preheated 200° oven. Turn off oven and let bowl stand for 6 to 24 hours or till mixture is firm when gently shaken. (You can discard the liquid that forms on top as the yogurt sets.)
	● After yogurt is firm, remove *2 tablespoons* to use as a starter for the next batch. Cover and store yogurt and starter up to 5 days in the refrigerator. Makes about 2 cups total.

Very Berry Yogurt: Prepare Homemade Yogurt as directed above. Stir together ½ cup crushed fresh or frozen-and-thawed *strawberries, raspberries, or blueberries* and 2 to 3 tablespoons *sugar or honey.* Gently fold into yogurt.

Cranberry-Orange Yogurt: Prepare Homemade Yogurt as directed above. Stir together ½ cup *cranberry-orange sauce* and 2 teaspoons *sugar.* Gently fold into yogurt.

Apple-Cinnamon Yogurt: Prepare Homemade Yogurt as directed above. Stir together 1 chopped medium *apple,* 2 tablespoons *brown sugar,* and ¼ teaspoon ground *cinnamon.* Gently fold into yogurt. Sprinkle with chopped *nuts,* if desired.

Lynn, one of our Test Kitchen home economists, became an expert yogurt maker thanks to this recipe. She discovered that the first batch of yogurt doesn't set as firmly as successive batches. So she suggests using your first batch as a starter for the next batch. (You may want to halve the recipe the first time since only a small amount is needed to start the next batch.)

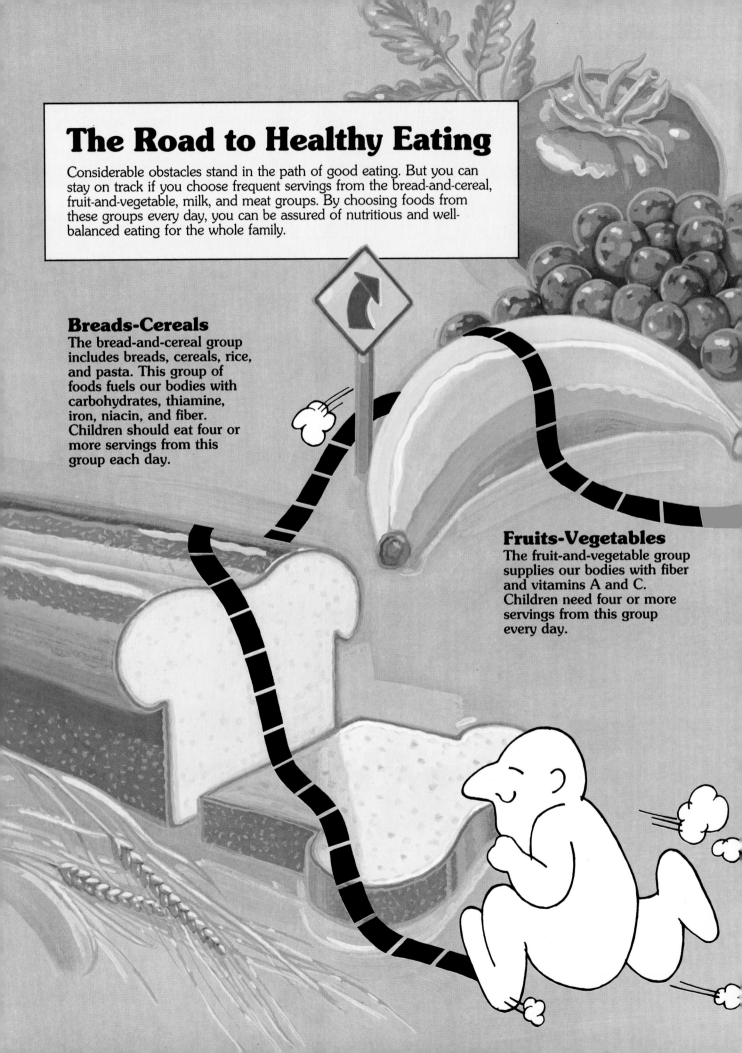

The Road to Healthy Eating

Considerable obstacles stand in the path of good eating. But you can stay on track if you choose frequent servings from the bread-and-cereal, fruit-and-vegetable, milk, and meat groups. By choosing foods from these groups every day, you can be assured of nutritious and well-balanced eating for the whole family.

Breads-Cereals

The bread-and-cereal group includes breads, cereals, rice, and pasta. This group of foods fuels our bodies with carbohydrates, thiamine, iron, niacin, and fiber. Children should eat four or more servings from this group each day.

Fruits-Vegetables

The fruit-and-vegetable group supplies our bodies with fiber and vitamins A and C. Children need four or more servings from this group every day.

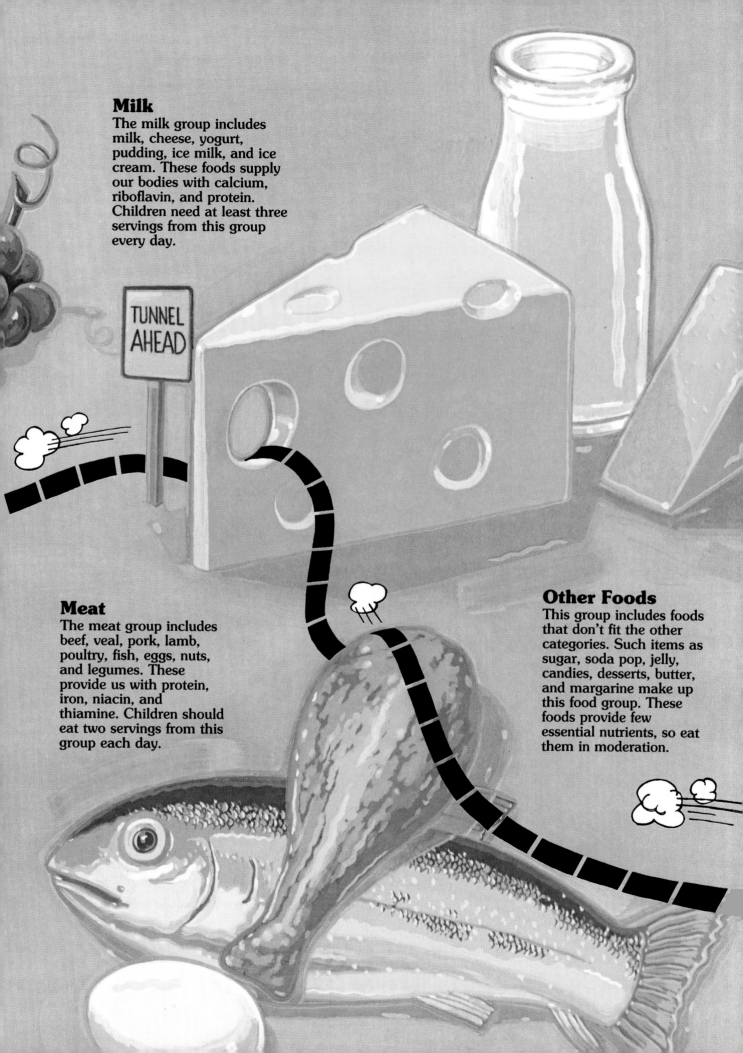

Milk

The milk group includes milk, cheese, yogurt, pudding, ice milk, and ice cream. These foods supply our bodies with calcium, riboflavin, and protein. Children need at least three servings from this group every day.

TUNNEL AHEAD

Meat

The meat group includes beef, veal, pork, lamb, poultry, fish, eggs, nuts, and legumes. These provide us with protein, iron, niacin, and thiamine. Children should eat two servings from this group each day.

Other Foods

This group includes foods that don't fit the other categories. Such items as sugar, soda pop, jelly, candies, desserts, butter, and margarine make up this food group. These foods provide few essential nutrients, so eat them in moderation.

	MILK GROUP	MEAT GROUP	FRUIT-VEGETABLE GROUP	BREAD-CEREAL GROUP
BREAKFAST				
Oatmeal (½ cup)				✔
Milk (1 cup)	✔			
Pumpkin Muffins*				✔
Orange juice (½ cup)			✔	
LUNCH				
Peanut butter sandwich		✔		✔ ✔
Dunk 'n' Munch Veggies*			✔	
Fruit juice (½ cup)			✔	
SNACK				
Popcorn				
DINNER				
Hamburger (2 oz. cooked)		✔		
Whole wheat bun				✔ ✔
Parmesan Potato Crisps*			✔	
Broccoli (½ cup)			✔	
Milk (1 cup)	✔			
Fresh Fruit Sippers*	✔			
DAILY TOTALS	**3**	**2**	**5**	**6**

See recipes, opposite and page 78

Check out our sample menu for a whole day of good eating. We show you how easy it is to eat well-balanced meals simply by choosing a variety of foods from each group.

Pumpkin Muffins

1½ cups whole wheat flour ½ cup all-purpose flour 1½ teaspoons baking powder ½ teaspoon baking soda ½ teaspoon ground cinnamon ¼ teaspoon salt ¼ teaspoon ground cloves ¼ teaspoon ground nutmeg	● Stir together whole wheat flour, all-purpose flour, baking powder, baking soda, cinnamon, salt, cloves, and nutmeg. Set aside.
2 slightly beaten eggs 1 cup canned pumpkin ½ cup sugar ½ cup milk ¼ cup cooking oil 1 cup raisins ½ cup broken *or* chopped walnuts	● In a large mixing bowl stir together eggs, pumpkin, sugar, milk, and cooking oil. Stir flour mixture into pumpkin mixture, stirring just till dry ingredients are moistened (batter should be lumpy). Fold in raisins and walnuts. Grease muffin cups or line with paper bake cups; fill ¾ full. Bake in a 400° oven about 15 minutes or till golden brown. Makes 18 muffins.

Don't wait till Halloween to enjoy these pumpkin muffins bursting with raisins. Start the day healthfully by serving them for breakfast with hot cereal and juice.

Dunk 'n' Munch Veggies

½ cup plain low-fat yogurt
½ cup dairy sour cream
¼ cup snipped parsley
2 tablespoons finely
    chopped green onion
¼ teaspoon dried dillweed
⅛ teaspoon garlic *or* onion
    powder
	● For dip, in a mixing bowl stir together yogurt, sour cream, parsley, green onion, dillweed, and garlic or onion powder. Cover and chill.

Assorted vegetable
    dippers (carrot, celery,
    or zucchini sticks;
    cherry tomatoes; *or*
    cauliflower *or* broccoli
    flowerets)
	● Serve vegetable dippers with chilled dip. Makes about 1¼ cups dip or 5 (¼-cup) servings.

If you're carrying this zesty dip in a brown bag or lunch box, pack it with a frozen box of juice or an ice pack to keep it cold.

Parmesan Potato Crisps

3 *or* 4 small baking potatoes 2 teaspoons margarine, melted	● Scrub potatoes; thinly slice (you should have 2 cups sliced potatoes). Arrange potatoes in a thin layer in a lightly greased 15x10x1-inch baking pan. Brush with melted margarine.	**Our version of homemade potato chips was a smashing success with the kid testers who gobbled them down. Soren said he could eat a sackful.**
¼ cup grated Parmesan cheese Dash pepper	● Sprinkle cheese and pepper over potatoes. Bake, uncovered, in a 450° oven for 18 to 20 minutes or till potatoes are brown and crisp. Serves 4.	

Fresh Fruit Sippers

1 pint vanilla ice milk 1 cup milk 1 small banana, cut into chunks; 1 medium peach, sliced; *or* ½ cup strawberries	● In a blender container place ice milk, milk, and fruit. Cover and blend till smooth. Pour into glasses. Makes 4 (5-ounce) servings.	**Vary the flavor of this high-calcium sipper with different fruit. Try it with bananas, peaches, or strawberrries.**

Index